THE PEOPLES AND CIVILIZATIONS
OF THE AMERICAS BEFORE CONTACT

ESSAYS ON GLOBAL AND COMPARATIVE HISTORY

A Series Edited by Michael Adas

Other titles in the series:
The Age of Gunpowder Empires, 1450–1800, William H. McNeill
The Columbian Voyages, the Columbian Exchange, and Their Historians,
    Alfred W. Crosby
Gender and Islamic History, Judith E. Tucker
Gender, Sex, and Empire, Margaret Strobel
The Hellenistic Period in World History, Stanley M. Burstein
"High" Imperialism and the "New" History, Michael Adas
Industrialization and Gender Inequality, Louise A. Tilly
Interpreting the Industrial Revolution, Peter N. Stearns
Islamic History as Global History, Richard M. Eaton
Shapes of World History in Twentieth-Century Scholarship,
    Jerry H. Bentley
The Silk Road: Overland Trade and Cultural Interactions in Eurasia,
    Xinru Liu
The Tropical Atlantic in the Age of the Slave Trade, Philip D. Curtin
The World System in the Thirteenth Century: Dead-End or Precursor?
    Janet Lippman Abu-Lughod

THE PEOPLES AND CIVILIZATIONS OF THE AMERICAS BEFORE CONTACT

JOHN E. KICZA

With a Foreword by Michael Adas, Series Editor

American Historical Association
Washington, D.C.

JOHN E. KICZA is Edward R. Meyer Distinguished Professor of History at Washington State University.

AHA editor: Amy Smith Bell

© 1998 American Historical Association

All rights reserved. No part of this book may be reproduced in any form without permission in writing from the publisher, except by a reviewer who wishes to quote brief passages in connection with a review written for inclusion in a magazine or newspaper.

Published in 1998 by the American Historical Association. As publisher, the American Historical Association does not adopt official views on any field of history and does not necessarily agree or disagree with the views expressed in this book.

Library of Congress Cataloging-in-Publication Data

Kicza, John E., 1947–
   The peoples and civilizations of the Americas before contact / John E. Kicza.
     p. cm. — (Essays on global and comparative history)
   Includes bibliographical references (p.).
   ISBN 0-87229-103-0 (pbk.)
   1. Indians—History. 2. Indians—Social life and customs. 3. Indians—Antiquities. 4. America—Antiquities. I. Title. II. Series.
E58.K53   1998
970.01—dc21   98-11234
                                                                                                            CIP

Printed in the United States of America

CONTENTS

Foreword   vi

1. THE COMING OF HUMANKIND TO THE AMERICAS   1
   The Gradual Agricultural Revolution   2
   The Olmecs: The Founding Civilization of Mesoamerica   5

2. CLASSIC CIVILIZATIONS OF CENTRAL MEXICO   9
   Teotihuacán Civilization   10
   Classic Mayan Civilization   12

3. THE END OF THE CLASSIC PERIOD   17
   The Toltecs: A Short-Lived Civilization of Broad Influence   18
   The Aztecs: Inheritors of Ancient Mesoamerican Traditions   21

4. EARLY CIVILIZATIONS OF THE ANDES   27
   Tiahuanaco and Huari: Precursors of the Incan Empire   29
   The Kingdom of Chimor: The Final Coastal Civilization   30
   The Incan Empire: The First Extensive Andean Civilization   31

5. IMPORTANT ATTRIBUTES OF SEDENTARY
   AND SEMISEDENTARY SOCIETIES   37
   Characteristics of Sedentary Imperial Civilizations   37
   The Great Number and Variety of Semisedentary Peoples   43
   The Population of the Americas on the Eve of European Contact   49

6. CONCLUSION   51

Notes   53

Bibliography   57

Foreword

Given the previously rather peripheral position of global and comparative history in the discipline, the growth of interest in these fields over the past three decades or so has been truly remarkable. The appearance of numerous works by prominent scholars on transcultural interaction and on variations in social systems and political economies, the great proliferation at both the college and secondary school levels of world history courses and numerous textbooks with which to teach them, and the formation in recent years of the World History Association, an affiliate of the American Historical Association, all testify to the increasing importance of global and comparative scholarship and teaching within the historical profession. In some ways these developments represent a revival, for world or cross-cultural history is as ancient as Herodotus, and it enjoyed particular favor among Western intellectuals from the eighteenth to the early twentieth centuries. But challenges to the grand designs or underlying "laws" that writers like Spengler or Toynbee discerned in human history, as well as an increasing emphasis on area specialization within the discipline as a whole, led to doubts about the feasibility or even the advisability of attempting to generalize across vast swaths of time and space. In scholarship, world history came to be seen as a pastime for dilettantes or popularists; in teaching, it was increasingly equated with unfocused social studies courses at the secondary school level.

Though the current interest in global history reflects a continuing fascination with the broad patterns of human development across cultures that were the focus for earlier works on world history, the "new" global or world history differs in fundamental ways from its predecessors. Writers of the new global history are less concerned with comprehensiveness or with providing a total chronology of human events. Their works tend to be thematically focused on recurring processes like war and colonization or on cross-cultural patterns like the spread of disease, technology, and trading networks. Their works are often more consciously and systematically comparative than the studies of earlier world historians. Partly because the research of area specialists has provided today's scholars with a good deal more data than was available to earlier writers, the best recent works on global history also display a far greater sensitivity than the more comprehensive world surveys to cultural nuances and the intricacies of the internal histories of the societies they cover. In addition, few practitioners of the new global history see their task as one of establishing universal "laws" or of identifying an overall teleological meaning in human development. Rather, their main concerns are the study of recurring processes and the dynamics and effects of cross-cultural interaction. Depending on their original area orientation, global and comparative historians adopt these approaches because they see them as the most effective way of bringing the experience of the "people without history" into the mainstream of teaching and scholarship, of relating the development of Europe to that of the rest of the world, or of challenging the misleading myth of exceptionalism that has dominated so much of the work on the history of the United States.

This series of essays is intended to provide an introduction to the new world history. Each pamphlet explores some of the interpretations and understandings that have resulted from cross-cultural and comparative historical studies undertaken in the past three or four decades. The pamphlets are designed to assist both college and secondary school teachers who are engaged in teaching courses on world history or courses with a comparative format. Each essay is authored by an expert on the time period or process in question. Though brief lists of works that teachers might consult for more detailed information on the topic covered are included in each of the pamphlets, the essays are not intended to be bibliographic surveys. Their central aim is to provide teachers facing the formidable task of preparing courses that are global or cross-cultural in scope with a sense of some of the issues that have been of interest to scholars working in these areas in recent decades. The essays deal with specific findings and the debates these have often generated, as well as broad patterns that cross-cultural study has revealed and their implications for the history of specific societies. Although all of the essays are thematically oriented, some are organized around particular historical eras like the age of Islamic expansion or the decades of industrialization, while others are focused on key topics like slavery or revolution.

Because there are many approaches to global history, these essays vary in format and content, from ones that are argumentative and highly interpretive to others that concentrate on giving an overview of major patterns or processes in global development. Each essay, however, suggests some of the most effective ways of dealing with the topic or the era covered, given the current state of our knowledge. In recognition of the quincentenary of Columbus's "discovery" of the Americas, the series begins with an essay on the impact of the processes set in motion by his voyages. Subsequent pamphlets cover topics and time periods from the era of early European overseas expansion to the present and then from the era of expansion back to the time of the Neolithic Revolution.

MICHAEL ADAS
Series Editor
Professor of History
Rutgers University

1

The Coming of Humankind to the Americas

H UMANS REACHED THE AMERICAS AT LEAST TWELVE THOUSAND YEARS ago, and possibly some thousands of years before that—perhaps as early as twenty-five thousand years before the modern era. There are surprisingly few artifacts that may precede the later date, and their precise dating has continued to be problematic in some significant way or another. Still, there is good reason to expect that the arrival date of humans in the western hemisphere may be pushed back significantly and reliably by new findings or dating techniques over the next quarter century. Migrants seem to have come largely across the region now identified as the Bering Strait (a land sometimes called *Beringia*), which at that time was totally or substantially dry because of the lower sea levels caused by the Ice Age.* Evidence indicates that these migrants came from different parts of East Asia, which at that time was receiving a substantial influx of peoples, in at least two major waves of migration. They dispersed rather rapidly across both continents, reaching the southern tip some ten thousand to eleven thousand years ago. For thousands of years these peoples subsisted as hunting bands pursuing primarily large game animals.

---

* Throughout this essay, geographic features and locales are identified by their modern names, names that did not necessarily exist at the time in which they are being discussed herein.

No compelling evidence indicates any contact other than incidental with societies from outside the Americas until Columbus's 1492 voyage. Genetic codes do not link these Native Americans to any non-Asian peoples, and the vast majority of cultural similarities lack specificity and could readily have developed independently. Indeed, the roughly simultaneous development of such significant advances as agriculture, pottery, and certain tools and weapons in distinct, widely separate zones in the Americas seems more in need of explanation than any perceived comparability with items or techniques from other parts of the globe.

The best documented connection of the Native Americans to any other peoples before the fifteenth century is the Viking voyages across the North Atlantic around A.D. 1000. Ships almost certainly reached Newfoundland at least several times, and the Vikings set up some sort of rudimentary coastal settlement for at least a short while. Nonetheless, the peoples of that area did not integrate any of the newcomers' practices into their cultural repertoire and seemingly entered into conflict with them. And as the Viking visit did not reverberate throughout the culture or history of Native American peoples, neither did it through that of European societies. The Norse produced few written records, and they raided other European societies more than they traded or otherwise interacted with them. Knowledge of the people on the other side of the Atlantic faded rapidly and thus played no role in the advent of European exploration across the Atlantic at the end of the fifteenth century.

THE GRADUAL AGRICULTURAL REVOLUTION

The commonly held view that the emergence of agriculture engendered a sharp disruption in the way of life of the peoples who adopted it may not be true in the case of the Americas. Some eight thousand years ago agriculture developed roughly simultaneously in at least four different zones in the Americas: coastal Peru, south-central Mexico, northeastern Mexico, and the southwestern United States. This simultaneity indicates that these diverse and widely separated peoples may have been responding to a common climatic shift. Although cultivation spread rapidly among neighboring societies in each of these distinct zones, little evidence hints at diffusion among them. But in all cases the coming of agriculture did not soon lead to nucleated settlement. Rather, various peoples seem to have long remained primarily hunters and gatherers, who planted some seeds at sites where they regularly encountered certain grains. Some forty-five hundred years passed before permanent communities emerged in either Mesoamerica (the region of central Mexico, southern Mexico, and Guatemala that shared quite comparable high cultures) or the Andean zone.

The first cultivated foods in the three northern sites were amaranth, accompanied by sunflowers in the southwestern United States and pumpkins in northeastern Mexico. Coastal Peruvian peoples initially raised nuts. Chile peppers were also developed very early on in several locations. These crops are completely different from those first cultivated in the Old World, which undercuts any argument that agriculture was introduced into the New World from the Old. Only later did native societies begin to grow the three crops that eventually came to dominate their diets: maize, manioc, and potatoes, each of which was cultivated in separate zones. Maize, grown in the same fields as beans and squashes, first appeared in Mesoamerica about seven thousand years ago.

Maize cultivation also flourished in coastal Peru but not in the Andean highlands, where residents relied on a tuber rather than a grain: the potato. And throughout eastern South America and in much of the Caribbean, the primary crop was manioc, a starchy tuber that when soaked, dried, grated into a flour, and baked yielded a nutritious though somewhat bland bread. In all cases, these three primary crops were accompanied by others that in combination produced well-rounded diets.

Maize cultivation in the early American societies rendered more calories per acre than did rice in East Asia or wheat and barley in Europe. Agriculture during this period in the Americas has wrongly been characterized as primitive when compared with that in Europe because of European use of draft animals and plows. But it certainly was not primitive when one considers that despite such deficiencies, these Native American societies regularly produced substantial food surpluses, which were sufficient to support large populations, considerable urbanization, and specialized occupations that were unassociated with agriculture. Furthermore, the peoples of the New World put more plants under cultivation than did those of the Old. Most agricultural societies in the Americas developed complementary food cultigens that in combination were nutritionally complete. This was a compelling need, because many native societies lacked animals that were suitable protein sources. Only the Andean zone contained animals—camelids—with substantial edible flesh, although other societies consumed turkeys and small dogs. The North American Plains Indians, of course, based their way of life totally around buffalo hunting and did not complement it with crop cultivation. In addition, the coastal and Amazon River basin peoples extensively used fish protein. In fact, they may have stressed the somewhat less nutritious crop of manioc as their primary cultigen because the waters yielded such large amounts of fish.

The successful storage techniques of Native American peoples further counter the argument that their agriculture was more primitive than that of the Old World. All communities in permanently sedentary zones maintained storehouses. Such expansionist peoples as the Aztecs and the Incas located storehouses throughout their territories to support armies as they campaigned. The Incas also supplied waystations and systems of runners along their thousands of miles of roads. The Andean peoples were the most advanced in food preservation techniques, actually turning their harsh climate into an advantage. Very early on, they learned how to freeze and dry potatoes and animal flesh into foods (*chuña* and *charqui*) with extremely long lifespans. (In the colonial period, plantation slaveowners throughout the Atlantic zone imported large amounts of dried meat from the South American *pampas,* or extensive plains, to feed their slaves inexpensively. Those in English-speaking regions could not pronounce *charqui* and came to call it "beef jerky" and eventually "jerked beef," totally misrepresenting the manner in which it is manufactured.)

Native Americans did face a very restrictive limitation on their promotion of agricultural production, however: suitable land. Both Mesoamerica and the Andean region are characterized by steep mountainsides and infertile soil, except along the occasional river valley, which is typically narrow rather than broad. An additional restriction is the sparse or at least irregular rainfall that many areas receive. Lacking large animals, Native American peoples could not use manure to fertilize fields (although the Peruvians made use of bird dung for this purpose), and lacking plows, they could not cultivate difficult soils or turn weeds underground. To expand agricultural production, they thus turned to massive public-works undertakings to greatly increase the amount of land they could cultivate.

The earliest major agricultural engineering projects were irrigation systems, generally small and local in Mesoamerica and much more massive in coastal Peru. Several thousand years ago, both regions contained sophisticated irrigation complexes. The Mayas, who began to coalesce into a civilization about two thousand years ago, used raised fields along human-made canals to vastly augment their agricultural output. The highland Andean peoples terraced many forbidding mountainsides, and then often irrigated the resultant fields. In the high plain (*altiplano*) adjacent to Lake Titicaca, local people constructed shallow canals around raised fields to use the fog that appeared during cold nights to protect the crops from frost damage. As the Valley of Mexico increasingly became the center of Mesoamerica over the roughly five hundred years before the coming of the Spaniards, the people residing around the massive lake complex and on the several islands within it developed the *chinampa* technique, which involved constructing small islands along the shores (they never "floated") that were cultivated intensively. Constantly receiving nutrients from the surrounding water, chinampas rendered two, and sometimes three, substantial harvests a year. (Indians continued to cultivate chinampas on the outskirts of Mexico City until at least the early nineteenth century.)

About thirty-five hundred years ago, permanently sedentary communities emerged in both Mesoamerica and the Andean zone. Completely reliant on agriculture for their sustenance, these societies underwent dramatic population growth with attendant occupational and social differentiation. Agriculture in these areas yielded reliable, substantial food surpluses, enabling a minority of men in each community to become full-time craft specialists, transporters and traders, priests, and professional military men. Permanent local nobilities and ruling families arose in each ethnic province. Massive, organized warfare emerged as these city-states fought over control of certain prized commodities and craft goods. Conflict also emerged over gaining privileged access to conquered lands and to the labor of subjugated peoples. Some of the most important provinces supported large cities: urban areas with populations in the tens of thousands were not unusual, and a couple of areas with several hundred thousand inhabitants appeared in Mexico, the most densely settled region in the pre-Hispanic Americas. These sedentary societies also constructed monumental architecture—palaces, pyramids, and temples—and elaborate, exquisitely erected ceremonial and governmental complexes.

THE OLMECS:
THE FOUNDING CIVILIZATION OF MESOAMERICA

Some three thousand years ago, the first civilization emerged in Mesoamerica—not in the central highlands, but along the gulf coast lowlands about midway between central Mexico and the Yucatán Peninsula. These people have been termed the Olmec, and their sophisticated culture prospered for more than eight hundred years, laying the base for the civilizations that followed in both central and southern Mexico. The Olmecs seem to have used two economic advantages to their great benefit. First, the region's soil was regularly flooded by several rivers that laid down high-quality silt with each flood. Hence, the Olmecs could generally harvest their crops twice a year, obtaining a food surplus unattained by other of their contemporaries. Second, they established the region as the center for the elaboration of fine stones, particularly jades, which were marketed throughout central and southern Mexico. Throughout its history, Mesoamerica has been characterized by market centers and trading networks, and the Olmecs advanced the practice of both. As would subsequent states, they employed military measures to enhance their trading advantages, using long-distance merchants as advance agents of their military and using the military to open new arenas of commerce.

The coastal lowland region inhabited by the Olmecs was much healthier than one might suppose after contact. Their agricultural practices produced greater surpluses than did those of their contemporaries (and their diet was already well rounded). Yellow fever (introduced later by the European expansion) and probably malaria (seemingly brought in through the same manner) were unknown. At the height of their civilization, the Olmecs numbered about three hundred and fifty thousand but unlike their successor states, they did not develop significant urban complexes. Instead, the Olmecs remained substantially rural and dispersed, and they centered their culture around three extensive and complex ceremonial sites, the first of any sophistication in Mesoamerica: La Venta, San Lorenzo, and Tres Zapotes.

The Olmecs had moved beyond tribal organization to state structures, having both occupational and political hierarchies, although currently there is no compelling reason to think that they had ever organized themselves into a single government or maintained a stable and enduring empire. Despite this, Olmec rulers were able to mobilize vast numbers of workers decade after decade to construct these massive ceremonial sites, which stretched over hundreds of yards and included mounds, pyramids, altars, extensive level areas, and elaborate mosaic floors. Most striking about Olmec artistry, however, is its carved stone structures. These huge heads and stelae were carved out of individual basalt boulders, some of which weighed more than twenty tons, and were transported by boat and overland from quarries some fifty miles away.

The Olmecs developed calendrical systems and the counting system, which would prevail among all subsequent civilizations in Mesoamerica, and they also had begun to use glyphs as mnemonics and incipient writing systems. The "Calendar Round" was based on a cycle of fifty-two years, which resulted from the overlap of two different day-count systems, one ritual and the other solar. The ritual cycle consisted of thirteen months (each with its own name) of twenty days, while the solar or "annual" calendar was composed of eighteen months of twenty days, plus an additional five days. The interplay of these two systems assured that any day in either system would intersect each fifty-two years. This may have been the basis of the cyclical view of history prevalent among both the Aztecs and the Mayas more than two thousand years later, for they expected the repetition of essential patterns involving such phenomena as the fortunes of royal dynasties and military invasions. And by at least late in Olmec history—about two thousand years ago—they had laid out the "Long Count" and recorded some dates according to it. For reasons unknown, the Long Count begins its calendar on August 13, 3114 B.C., and records later dates from it, using a vigesimal system of counting that used a bar to represent "five" and a dot to represent "one." A shell-like character represented "zero."

The Olmecs also seem to have been the first people to play the "Ball Game." Called *tlachtli* in Nahuatl, the Aztec language, the Ball Game utilized a large court shaped like a capital "I," with sloping sides. Individuals or teams sought to hit a rubber ball to their opponent's end of the court without using their hands or feet to strike the ball. Tremendously popular, these games attracted many spectators who gambled heavily. On occasion, the games were viewed as representing struggles between gods. Carvings on the stone walls of some courts depict the losing team's captain being decapitated. Remains of courts exist today not only throughout Mesoamerica but also on major Caribbean islands and in the desert vastness of northern Mexico.

The Olmec civilization experienced conflict and decline as early as 400 B.C., when La Venta shows signs of defacement and conflagration. Reasons for the violence—whether an internal uprising or an invasion—remain unknown. Although Tres Zapotes survived at least to some extent for another four hundred years, no ceremonial site truly thrived during that time. At its end, the Olmec civilization abandoned these sites, and its state organization fragmented into individual communities that relied on slash-and-burn agriculture. Coordinated, large-scale agricultural production seems to have ceased with the violent collapse of the state structure—a process that may have prefigured the collapse of the Mayan civilization farther south some nine hundred years later.

2

Classic Civilizations of Central Mexico

THE CLASSIC PERIOD, WHICH RUNS FROM THE BEGINNING OF THE CHRISTIAN era to about A.D. 900, witnessed a flowering of distinct high civilizations throughout most of Mesoamerica, with many fundamental traits derived directly from the Olmecs. The population of Mesoamerica expanded dramatically early in the period, evidence that various peoples were making widespread use of irrigation, terracing, raised fields, and other forms of agricultural engineering. A vast number of elaborate sites arose, each one a complex of significant ceremonial and residential structures. Tremendous urbanization characterized the epoch. A well-articulated social hierarchy evolved throughout the entire culture zone. The Calendar Round spread throughout Mesoamerica, but only the Mayas adopted the Long Count. At least four of the major civilizations incorporated similar but unique glyphic writing systems. The most acclaimed of these civilizations are Teotihuacán of the Valley of Mexico and the Mayas of the greater Yucatán Peninsula. But sole emphasis on their magnificence results in a relative ignorance of remarkable complexes in other regions, particularly El Tajín in Veracruz and Monte Albán in Oaxaca. A brief consideration of Monte Albán illustrates the accomplishments of a "secondary" Classic civilization.

Monte Albán first became prominent around 400 B.C. as a ceremonial complex and true urban center—already with a population of five thousand people—on a leveled hilltop in the middle of the Valley of Oaxaca.

This capital of the Zapotec people prospered largely without disruption, reaching a population of about thirty thousand until A.D. 900, when it went into rapid decline and was soon abandoned. The slopes of the hill contained a few thousand residential terraces. Intensive irrigation throughout the surrounding lowlands provided the nutrition for this urban complex. The ceremonial site itself contained numerous large buildings of diverse styles scattered around a central plaza. About 175 subterranean tombs have been discovered so far throughout the site, a number of them magnificent in construction and containing finely crafted items, many of precious metals.

TEOTIHUACÁN CIVILIZATION

Around the beginning of the Christian era, Teotihuacán (situated in a northeastern branch of the Valley of Mexico) developed commercial and cultural preeminence throughout central Mexico and even into some areas as far south as Guatemala and as far north as the southwestern United States. It likewise conducted successful campaigns of conquest and politically subjugated substantial parts of central Mexico, demanding tribute and labor service from the conquered provinces. Teotihuacán proper, covering nine square miles, became the largest urban complex in Mesoamerica until the Aztec capital of Tenochtitlán virtually matched its size some eight hundred years later: both cities attained populations of at least two hundred thousand, perhaps as large as two hundred and fifty thousand. Teotihuacán was organized into residential compounds surrounded by walls, each of which seemingly contained a lineage group. The importance of commerce to the city is illustrated by one ward of the city that consisted of merchants from the Mayan and coastal lowland areas. The rulers dwelled in palace compounds. One structure in the city, the Ciudadela, measures more than 640 meters a side. The street that runs through the heart of the city is abutted by two vast pyramids: the Pyramid of the Sun and the Pyramid of the Moon. The city is replete with stone carvings, and the walls of the most important structures are still decorated with bright frescoes.

The Teotihuacán community worshiped a pantheon of gods, which would persist with little variation through the era of the Aztecs a millennium later. This pantheon included the Rain God, the Plumed Serpent, the Flayed One, the Sun God, and the Moon God—a few of the most prominent of a much longer list. The character of this pantheon was much the same from culture to culture in Mesoamerica, but the names of each deity might vary from one ethnic province to another, and each might be endowed with certain local characteristics along with universal ones.

Some of Teotihuacán's wealth and preeminence derived from its crucial role in long-distance commerce of precious items, particularly obsidian (the sharp, easily hewn volcanic stone that served as the primary source of blades and points in Mesoamerica in the absence of industrial metals). The city contained at least three hundred and fifty obsidian workshops. During Teotihuacán's domination of the Central Mexican culture zone, Mesoamerica's influence began to reach extensively into the desert north, a process that would endure well beyond the city's collapse. Cultural traits that penetrated into the arid regions of the north include pyramids, I-shaped ball courts, promotion of the religious cult of Quetzalcoatl (the Plumed Serpent), and an elaborate road system. Society also became more structured and elaborate. Charles C. Di Peso has remarked about the relationship between these two zones:

> These various Southern Periphery trading centers flourished only because of specific Mesoamerican sponsorship, for study of their individual emplacements indicates the presence of the Mesoamerican *pochteca* [long-distance merchants] exploitative strategy in terms of natural resources and available manpower. These frontier traders were probably held responsible for supplying certain amounts of luxury goods, such as turquoise and perhaps peyote, to the home merchants for the initial cost of their emplacement. It is well known that Mesoamerican trader families effected a market organization somewhat resembling certain economic aspects of the Hudson's Bay or Dutch East Indies companies. It is obvious that these leaders moved their Chichimec [a Nahuatl term for the nonsedentary peoples of the desert north] wards to a sociocultural level where they became capable of producing an agricultural surplus for trading, mining, and other profitable extracting industries, including slaving.[1]

Teotihuacán reached its zenith in the fifth and sixth centuries. Although it would survive intact for another two centuries, its scope began to recede after this period. Oaxaca, for example, showed none of its influence after the sixth century. In the mid-eighth century Teotihuacán was successfully invaded by desert societies from the north. Some of its most notable structures that remain today show signs of burning and desecration. Teotihuacán was abandoned, and its people scattered into surrounding small communities. An early colonial Nahuatl source refers to the city's leaders departing and taking with them "the writings, the books, the paintings; they carried away all the crafts, the castings of metals."[2]

Classic Mayan Civilization

Far to the south, in the greater Yucatán Peninsula, the Mayas instituted transforming improvements in their agricultural techniques and expanded their long-distance trade at roughly the same time as did Teotihuacán. But unlike that city, the lowland Mayas never developed a centralized empire. Instead, they organized themselves into a group of rival provincial powers of similar attainments that frequently pursued warfare against each other. (The highland Mayas of central Guatemala and Chiapas never rivaled the accomplishments of their lowland counterparts to the north.) About a dozen of these states were ruled by monarchs in the first century B.C.; perhaps sixty were so governed at the height of Mayan civilization in the eighth century. But they faced no external threats, unlike the empires of central Mexico. When Mayan civilization collapsed in the ninth century, it did so as a consequence of internal disruptions.

The economic accomplishments of the Mayas over the millennium preceding A.D. 900 are even more remarkable than that of the peoples of central Mexico, because the Mayan environment and climate posed much harsher challenges. The level limestone peninsula leeched the thin soil of its nutrients and the tropical climate fostered the growth of plants and bush, which always threatened the land cleared for agriculture. The slash-and-burn cultivation (practiced early in Mayan history and then again after the civilization's collapse) could not sustain the population required to construct the many ceremonial centers that arose during the Classic period and the political and religious elites and specialized craftsmen who resided there.

Over the past twenty years scholars have begun to explain this enigma through closer examination of ancient agricultural practices. They have found that the lowland Mayas of the Classic period made great use of hydraulic and raised-field systems to increase the amount of land under cultivation and its yields. Scholars estimate that the lowland Mayas numbered between three million and five million people, more than double the number on the peninsula upon the arrival of the Spaniards some six centuries after the civilization's collapse. (The Mayan achievements in the Classic period were so long past and forgotten by the native people that most of these elaborate sites were not even discovered by the Spaniards in the colonial period.)

The Classic Mayas participated in commerce and interacted with the societies of central Mexico far more than scholars once thought. Indications are that Mayan-speaking groups resided in several different zones in highland Mexico during the Classic period. Various sites bear their cultural stamp, in both designs and carved symbolic glyphs. Symbols and goods from Teotihuacán proliferated in Tikal, one of the greatest Mayan centers on the peninsula. As noted previously, an entire neighborhood in Teotihuacán appears to have been devoted to merchants from the coastal lowlands.

The Mayas engaged in tremendous trade on the peninsula and into central Mexico, along the coast in large canoes, and perhaps even out to the larger islands of the Caribbean. Like many native societies, they dealt in precious stones such as jade, but they also traded specific coastal and lowland products, including salt, exquisite feathers, and cacao (greatly prized as a beverage in central Mexico).

Scholars once thought that the enormous ceremonial sites sustained only a small resident population, but they now appreciate that at least several sites contained populations in the tens of thousands and functioned as major trading centers, not just as religious and government centers. For at least several centuries, Tikal enjoyed a population of at least 30,000 people and perhaps more than 50,000; the site contains more than 3,000 structures on slightly more than six square miles. Copán had more than 20,000 inhabitants. The dozens of distinct provinces were characterized by rather elaborate centers surrounded by subordinate agricultural communities. Stuart J. Fiedel has described the layout of these complexes:

> A typical Classic center was composed of a series of stepped platforms surrounded by masonry superstructures, arranged around plazas or courtyards. At Tikal and other large centers, several such complexes were linked by causeways. The grandest structures were the tall, steep-sided temple pyramids, built of limestone blocks facing a rubble core. At Tikal there were six pyramids; the tallest of these rose to a height of 70 m. (229 ft.)....Besides pyramids, a typical complex included a number of lower platforms, which supported single-storey buildings with as many as several dozen rooms. Although they do not seem very comfortable, these structures are generally assumed to have been élite residences....Other structures commonly found in central complexes were ballcourts and reservoirs.[3]

Provinces conducted frequent warfare against each other, but any formal empires achieved were rather circumscribed and short-lived. Military success resulted in neither reliable tribute payments nor labor service delivery. Rather, combat seems to have been intended to add to the luster of the local ruling elites and their sponsoring gods and to resolve, at least temporarily, issues of cultural and commercial preeminence. The victors often inflicted torture and human sacrifice on defeated commanders.

Mayan cultural achievements include the construction of magnificent pyramids and stelae decorated with bas-reliefs of stone and wood. Walls were covered with colorful frescoes, only a few of which have survived. The Long Count calendar was widely used in the lowlands, but the Mayas took it to its highest refinement, commencing its use in the lowlands around A.D. 250. They seem not to have employed their sophisticated mathematical system for quotidian purposes such as recording amounts and values for storage and exchange. Rather, priests used the calendar for astronomical and astrological tracking. The few surviving pre-Hispanic documents indicate that their measurement of the lunar month was off by only seven minutes and that they kept close and regular track of Jupiter, Mars, Mercury, and Venus.

The Mayas of the Classic period also had a fully developed writing system. Michael D. Coe has commented:

> The Maya script was the only *complete* writing system in the ancient New World: that is, only the Maya could express in writing everything that was in their language. It was a complex mixture of ideographic and phonetic elements, similar in structure to certain scripts of the Old World, such as Sumerian, Egyptian and Japanese. Since the system included a complete syllabary (i.e., a symbol for each syllable), they could in theory have written everything phonetically, but like the Japanese they did not because the ideographs continued to have immense prestige and probably even religious overtones....Maya hieroglyphic writing appears on a wide variety of materials. From the last decade of the 3rd century A.D. until the Classic downfall, there are hundreds of inscriptions on stelae, wall panels, lintels, and other stone monuments which are now proven to be dynastic records, including the births, accessions to power, marriages, victories and deaths of the elite caste that ruled the lowland cities. There must have been thousands of codices—folding-screen books of bark paper coated with gesso—but all those of Classic date have disappeared, with only four surviving from the Post-Classic period. In addition, vast numbers of painted or carved funerary vases contain hieroglyphic texts, some as long as those on the monuments.[4]

After the collapse of the Classic civilization and the elimination of the priestly and provincial ruling classes (and the specialized class of scribes who served them) and the abandonment of the ceremonial sites, both the

Long Count and inscriptions in stone ceased. In the numerous agricultural communities that remained, however, local scribes sometimes continued to record local traditions and histories. This practice continued—largely surreptitiously—after the Spanish conquest, with the Roman alphabet eventually replacing native script in some cases. Only in recent years are scholars beginning to appreciate the richness of colonial documentation preserved in the Mayan language and what it tells us about the lives and values of these people.[5]

Reasons for the collapse of the Mayan civilization remain ultimately unknown, although scholars now have a better idea of some of the primary factors at play. The disintegration was certainly caused by reasons internal to the civilization, for there are no signs of invasion. This disintegration swept through the lowlands, and although ceremonial sites were not burned and ravaged, they were abandoned almost overnight, so much so that some carvings were left partially completed. The process of dissolution seems to have involved a vast increase in warfare, for a number of short-lived fortified communities have recently been discovered, usually located at some distance from traditional population centers and in relatively inaccessible areas. The result of the dissolution included the cessation of the Long Count calendar, the end of large-scale building of structures and monuments, and thus no further stone carvings depicting dynastic histories and religious beliefs. The ruling families and hierarchy of priests disappeared, repudiated by the commoners. And the scribes, long-distance merchants, and most craftsmen ceased to practice their trades. Lacking supervision, the major agricultural engineering improvements—canals and raised fields—fell into rapid disrepair. The Mayas largely reverted to swidden agriculture, causing their population to fall to a fraction of its former size. Most societies knew no political loyalty higher than the individual village. Efforts to erect provincial structures after A.D. 900 largely failed and every political coalition was unstable and ephemeral.

Markers indicate the pace of the decline: After 672 no new communities began to carve monuments; the civilization had ceased its expansion. After 751 traditional alliances began to break down and long-distance trade decreased. The number of wars seems to have increased. The year 889, which marks the end of a time cycle, is commemorated at only three sites. The last Long Count date recorded is 909.

The best evidence indicates that as the lowland Mayan population increased notably in the Classic period, greater demands were placed on the agricultural infrastructure, while the elite drew more people away from agricultural endeavors to work in their self-aggrandizing ventures and to fight for their glory. When famines, natural disasters, or military defeats transpired, the fatalism and the belief in human and natural cycles among the Mayas would have encouraged severe questioning and depression. In this setting, the leaders may well have responded by marshaling ever-larger armies, trying to remedy their individual plights by success in combat against rival provinces. But because the crisis was civilizationwide, no immediate and local victory could solve the deeper problem. The stress on the agricultural infrastructure could have been exacerbated by the more extensive warfare. These pressures could have brought on widespread famine, repudiation of the belief-structures inherent in the economically unproductive ceremonial cities and of the political and religious leaders, and flight into the backcountry, where smaller, subsistence-oriented communities emerged and persisted until the Europeans arrived. Long-distance trade routes shifted from the heartland of the peninsula to the coast, and those power centers that arose after the civilization's collapse did so away from the lowland zone and along the northern reaches of the Yucatán.

3

The End of the Classic Period

As evidenced by the failure of such dispersed and magnificent civilizations as Monte Albán, Teotihuacán, and Mayan, a widespread crisis brought the Classic period to an end throughout Mesoamerica between A.D. 700 and 900, after close to a millennium of cultural florescence. More was clearly involved than the coincidental collapse of a series of cultures of high achievement. Experts are in general agreement that some sort of environmental crisis drastically decreased agricultural productivity throughout central Mexico, sufficiently weakening the existing powers to make them vulnerable to invasion by societies from the desert north which had already been brought into the region's commercial circuit—and which may even have adopted agriculture to some extent. The decline and ultimate abandonment of Teotihuacán was the initial transforming event. The collapse of Monte Albán followed hard upon it. But although Teotihuacán's fall brought about a fragmentation of power, culture, and trading patterns throughout central Mexico, its immediate effect on the Mayan lowlands was to stimulate economic and cultural expansion. The Mayan civilization continued to prosper over the following two centuries.

The disappearance of Teotihuacán's civilization and empire eliminated a unifying political and commercial center in central Mesoamerica, but it did not disrupt settlement patterns, cultivation practices, or the region's fundamental organization into ethnic provinces. Major cities endured; Atzcapotzalco, Cholula, and Xochicalco are the most outstanding examples. The systems of agricultural engineering that supported the dense sedentary population throughout central Mexico persisted. The region's population seems to have maintained much of its size, as no widespread famine occurred and the level of warfare did not increase.

But as already noted, such was not the case among the Mayan civilization, in which all cities and ceremonial sites were abandoned. The state system that provided the coherence of ethnic provinces substantially broke down only to be resurrected sporadically and briefly in subsequent centuries. The agricultural engineering systems collapsed completely, with the loss of probably more than half of the region's population in a rather short period. This certainly was accompanied by waves of famine. So the Mayan civilization lost its organic structure, while that of central Mexico endured, although it lacked an integrating center for more than two centuries.

THE TOLTECS:
A SHORT-LIVED CIVILIZATION OF BROAD INFLUENCE

From A.D. 950 to 1150 the people known as the Toltecs based in their capital of Tula some forty miles north of Lake Texcoco in the Valley of Mexico, developed a small empire but a far more extensive shared culture and trade zone. They benefited from a stable, thriving agricultural setting, as their valley was crisscrossed with irrigation canals from the reliable Tula River. The Toltec population never approximated that of Teotihuacán; during the civilization's ascendancy, the inhabitants of Tula numbered only thirty thousand to sixty thousand, with a similar number in its immediate hinterland. It thus lacked a large army and seems to have directly controlled only the adjacent provinces in central Mexico. But its commerce—and as a consequence, its culture—extended from the Pueblo people in the southwestern United States (and even the southeast to some extent) down to the Yucatán Peninsula. Among the most common artifacts found in Tula were Maya-produced glazed pottery items that were imported to furnish elite Toltec households. Furthermore, around A.D. 900—just as the Toltec civilization was beginning to coalesce—some level of contact with the Andean zone resulted in the introduction of metallurgy into central Mexico. This connection seems to have not long persisted, but the Mexican peoples began to produce precious ornaments and copper tools in considerable amounts, though stone tools and weapons (particularly obsidian) remained dominant until the arrival of the Spanish.

In fact, the shaping of obsidian implements seems to have provided Tula with some of its importance. Its empire controlled the nearby obsidian mines of Pachuca, and perhaps 40 percent of the city's inhabitants devoted themselves to the production of obsidian tools and points. The

Toltecs also expanded commerce with societies of the desert north, which Teotihuacán had begun six centuries earlier. The north contained turquoise and other rare mineral mines; the people of the small northern site of Alta Vista shaped turquoise for trade with the south. Northern societies prized the cacao and feathers, which could be obtained only from southern Mexico. Other centers of importance—particularly Casas Grandes and La Quemada—developed in the desert north. Charles C. Di Peso has remarked about these elaborate sites:

> ...[T]hese Southern Periphery centers were marked by the sudden introduction of a definable cluster of Mesoamerican traits that could have been implanted by a few *pochteca*—for example, the comparatively rapid massing of people into population centers that were dependent upon intensive agriculture, extensive trade, and artisan specialization. Certainly, the recorded architecture associated with each of these organizations cannot have been derived from the indigenous culture base, which obviously lacked the technical know-how required to produce these Mesoamerican-like designs— the I-shaped ball court complex, truncated mounds, staircases, colonnades, hydraulic farming systems, and city water systems.[1]

Di Peso also noted that from very early on most of these centers "were strongly involved with the Mesoamerican Quetzalcoatl religious theme that seems to have been central to their stratified class systems."[2] Similar culture traits and figures spread among the agricultural societies in the southwestern United States. Significant Toltec influence is also apparent in the temple mound and ceremonial plazas found in the southeastern United States. But there, this cultural accretion only modified long-established patterns of site construction that had spread into the region from moundbuilding societies of the northern Mississippi River and Ohio River Valley (see chapter five for more on these societies).

The Toltecs themselves seem to have been composed of at least two different ethnic groups who came together from different directions, at least one of which had recently migrated from the north as one of these peoples who had only recently adopted the sedentary agricultural way of life. The polity was inherently unstable, as these disparate groups never smoothly combined. During the two-hundred-year history of the Toltec civilization, a disaffected—and perhaps repudiated—political leader named Ce Acatl Topiltzin Quetzalcoatl led a contingent of Toltecs into the northern Yucatán Peninsula, on the fringe of the region where Mayan civilization had collapsed several centuries before. There, they greatly expanded and reconfigured the center of Chichen Itza, designing it after the city of Tula, with many similar structures. They also introduced the cultural icon of Quetzalcoatl to the Mayan zone, where he was known as Kulkulcan. Chichen Itza developed a small empire, or at least a confederation, that endured for a couple of centuries. But as its rulers intermarried with Mayan noble families at an increasing rate, the site's distinctiveness and influence waned.

The history of central Mexico begins to be actively recorded with the Toltecs. Certainly earlier societies had written histories as well, but these records did not survive physically or as influences in later codices. From the founding of Tula until the coming of the Spanish, one can supplement archaeological evidence with information from native codices and with the historical memories of later indigenous writers. The documentation is so abundant that the ethnohistorian Nigel Davies has composed a three-volume history of central Mexico from the founding of Tula through the Aztec period.[3] But much of the history recorded was done for narrow dynastic interests and as overt propaganda to legitimize royal lineages, conquests, religious symbols, and the like. In her recent comparison of four Mesoamerican writing traditions, Joyce Marcus has remarked:

> From the very beginning, it seems likely that writing was a propaganda tool of the hereditary elite—either horizontal propaganda aimed at competing chiefs, vertical propaganda aimed at their subjects, or a combination of the two. Moreover, some of the themes seen in the earliest monuments with writing are ones that went on to be developed by later Mesoamerican states. Included were victory in battle; the sacrifice of prisoners; the placing of political events in a dated context; the naming of important persons for the day on which they were born; and the depiction of travel by human footprints.[4]

Histories thus contend with each other, and those that survive are sometimes in direct contradiction with one another. Only careful critical analysis can reconcile them, and even then not always.

The Toltec civilization fell around 1150; the process included active destruction and burning of some of the city. Evidence indicates that once again nonsedentary Chichimec peoples migrated from the desert north, probably impelled by an increasingly drier climate that had diminished their agricultural capacity. This was certainly not a "raid and return" operation; rather, these migratory peoples settled throughout central Mexico. Many of the peoples extant in that region when the Spanish arrived date their own arrival from this time or the following two centuries. Some societies were client states or mercenary forces for established provinces, but even some of the latter—most notably the Mexica (also known as the Tenochca), the primary member of the Triple Alliance that assembled the Aztec empire—date their arrival from this era. Michael D. Coe has described this process:

> Refugees from this center of Toltec civilization [Tula] managed to establish themselves in the southern half of the Valley [of Mexico], particularly at the towns of Colhuacan and Xico, both of which became important citadels transmitting the higher culture of their predecessors to the savage groups who were then streaming into the northern half. Among the latter were the band of Chichimeca under their chief Xolotl, arriving in the Valley by 1244 and settling at Tenayuca; the Acolhua, who founded Coatlinchan around the year 1260; the Otomí at Xaltocan by about 1250; and the powerful Tepanecs, who in 1230 took over the older town of Atzcapotzalco....Thus, by the thirteenth century, all over the Valley there had sprung up a group of modestly sized city-states, those in the north founded by Chichimec upstarts eager to learn from the Toltecs in the south.[5]

THE AZTECS:
INHERITORS OF ANCIENT MESOAMERICAN TRADITIONS

When the Mexica arrived in the Valley of Mexico in the early fourteenth century, they were late participants in a much larger phenomenon. Mexica legends assert that the Mexica wandered for two hundred years before reaching the Valley of Mexico. Upon arrival, they were relegated to living in the provinces of other ethnic groups and serving them as mercenary forces in the endemic warfare that then characterized central Mexico. Around 1325 the Mexica settled on an island in the middle of vast Lake Texcoco and began to construct the city of Tenochtitlán, which in 1478 incorporated its northern neighbor on the island, Tlatelolco. This canal-crossed, grid-style city was connected to the mainland by three causeways that were interspersed with removable bridges, which served two purposes: (1) to facilitate traffic by the thousands of canoes that traveled daily to and from the city and (2) to make the city virtually impregnable from attack. (The advantage of water transport was heightened in this zone that was so totally lacking in pack animals.) A lengthy aqueduct that ran west to the mainland provided the city with abundant potable water. The major city of Texcoco on the lake's east bank (later part of the Triple Alliance, along with the very junior third member of Tlacopan, also known as Tacuba) constructed a vast north-south dike east of Tenochtitlán to separate the rather saline waters of the eastern and northern sections of the lake from the much fresher waters of the western and southern sections. The Mexica used this fresh water to construct a vast complex of chinampas, which allowed year-round cultivation and provided a substantial portion of the food for this city, whose population eventually reached two hundred thousand to three hundred thousand.

The Mexica took great pride in being the most successful of all of the "savage" peoples who had migrated from the north, and they wrote considerably about their origins and evolution. They also cast themselves as the legitimate heirs of the Toltec culture, however, which was seen as the founding civilization of central Mexico. Knowledge of Teotihuacán had long disappeared, and the magnificent site endured unpopulated and a mystery to the region's peoples. Mexica rulers intermarried with surviving royal Toltec lineages as soon as they could, and the culture incorporated gods, rituals, and cultural styles from ancient Tula, even ransacking the city to gather religious artifacts to transfer to Tenochtitlán.

The Mexica had been installed in Tenochtitlán for more than a century and were still functioning as a client state to the Tepanec capital of Atzcapotzalco when in 1428 they led a successful rebellion against it (with crucial, if not decisive, assistance from Texcoco). Following this surprising victory, the Triple Alliance—led by the Mexica—rapidly assembled the Aztec empire, which had fully incorporated thirty-eight dependent provinces by 1519. It is important to note the relative youth of the Aztec empire at that date. It was barely ninety years old, and the subject provinces could readily remember their autonomy before the Aztec conquest. Although certainly the largest formal empire ever assembled in central Mexico, the Aztec empire bears fundamental similarities with the civilizations that preceded it. Nigel Davies has noted:

> The Empire was more a series of strong-points than a continuous domain. And if there was more emphasis on military conquest in Aztec times than before, this pattern of a central megalopolis, surrounded by its inner metropolitan area but also extending its influence, whether military or commercial, to distant places, recurs throughout the history of Middle America.[6]

The course and timing of Aztec expansion is well recorded. It seems to have been oriented more toward gaining privileged access—through tribute or at least unequal exchange—to scarce prized commodities, such as feathers, cacao (which was even used as a standard medium of exchange), and jade, than toward obtaining comestibles and other bulk items, although significant amounts of these were collected as well.

Long-distance trade remained important under the Aztecs, and their merchants were commonly used as spies and effectively as advance scouts of the empire. They sometimes offered provinces disadvantageous terms of trade, which if accepted, signified their peaceful incorporation into the imperial arrangement. Alternatively, a refusal or the killing of the merchants constituted a declaration of war. Perhaps encouraged by the relative peace imposed by the Aztecs, local and provincial markets prospered and proliferated throughout central Mexico. Some even had judges present on market days to resolve disputes on the spot. Aztec commerce extended well into what is now New Mexico, as the empire's merchants forged routes of communication different from those of Tula and Teotihuacán. They likewise promoted worship of Huitzilopochtli (Hummingbird on the Left), the central god in the Aztec pantheon, over the traditional devotion to Quetzalcoatl, who had been introduced centuries before into the region from Mesoamerica.

The empire was never contiguous, for certain mountainous and otherwise resource-scarce provinces were simply ignored, or if engaged in periodic battle, were never systematically invested. Also, the powerful Tarascan people of western Mexico at least twice easily overcame major Aztec invasions. The Aztec empire expected its dependent provinces to store food for possible use by its armies as they marched to the frontier or against rebellious subjects. The Triple Alliance always provided the core of the army, but it was routinely supplemented by contingents from subject states, which were commanded by their own leaders and kept their distinct identities. Conquered provinces were permitted to retain their traditional ethnic rulers, religion, and cultural identity, and they generally added one or more major Aztec gods to their pantheons, particularly as the success of the empire evidenced their efficacy. The Aztec leaders might seize for their own some lands previously owned by the defeated nobles, but otherwise, as long as a province did not rebel and regularly delivered tribute and labor service from its people, the conquerors interfered little with it.

The cultural symbols, crafts, architecture, and artistic styles of the Aztecs are all directly derivative of the civilizations that preceded them; likewise with their technology. Chinampa cultivation, after all, was practiced more than a millennium earlier; the Aztecs simply expanded it significantly in their lacustrine zone. Their tools and weapons were based on obsidian and other sharp minerals. Their use of metallurgy was limited and not well advanced. Over roughly two thousand years the peoples of central Mexico had implemented agricultural engineering to expand the amount of land under cultivation, but they had achieved little to make that land significantly more productive. Widespread famines occurred periodically. During a period of great imperial expansion, a horrible famine befell the Aztecs in the 1450s.

Perhaps what most distinguished the Aztecs from other Mesoamerican peoples, both their predecessors and contemporaries, was the scale of their practice of human sacrifice. The ritual execution of war captives, criminals, and unfortunates took place in every Mesoamerican civilization beginning with the Olmecs. As previously noted, the ritual surrounding the Ball Game sometimes included the execution of the losing captain. Mayan murals and raised carvings regularly depicted the torture of captured enemy soldiers and the sacrifice of their commanders. Further, as part of their religious practices, the Mayas, like other Mesoamerican cultures, inflicted the shedding of blood on themselves as well. Images depict royal men and women passing barbed strings through their tongues and other body parts to gather blood for offering to the gods.

The Aztecs transformed a common but limited practice into the central element of their religious ritual. They did so because they saw themselves as carrying a tremendous cosmic burden: the continued functioning of the world through appeasement of the gods, gods who had destroyed the world four times previously. They also devotedly followed the Calendar Round and thought that the world might end at the end of each fifty-two-year cycle. And their primary god, Huitzilopochtli, a sun god, might not come up in the morning or bless their warfare against others unless he was fueled with blood offered as the smoke from braziers containing the hearts that Aztec priests ripped out of victims stretched across their altars.

Blood sacrifice apparently became far more common throughout central Mexico in the time of the Aztecs. Other societies inflicted it on Aztec captives of their own, and the literature and oral memoirs from that era relate a belief that sacrificial victims joined the gods—or even became gods themselves—and supposed incidents in which societies repudiated captured members who did not die well (that is, with honor). The Aztecs recounted numerous exemplary orations by men about to die on the altar or in imitation combat that was rigged against them, stating their pride and glory in dying well as captives. Blood sacrifice was sometimes followed by ritual cannibalism of the victim's limbs, but never by his captor. The society believed that the victim's commendable attributes were thereby transferred to the consumer. Although some scholars have raised the question of whether this cannibalism was also conducted to provide actual nutrition, the bulk of the evidence overwhelmingly demonstrates that it was only ritual in character.

The Aztecs may well have reached the natural limits of their empire when the Spanish arrived in the early 1500s. They were not successful against the intransigent Tarascans, and the other unsubdued provinces within the empire's boundaries held little promise. Montezuma had an army in the south, poised to invade Mayan territory, but these scattered villages seemed to have little to offer their potential invaders—as the Spaniards would soon discover. The Aztec empire, though never rebellion-free, appeared quite intact and thriving. No indigenous invaders threatened the imperial center, and evidence shows no impending subsistence crisis or crisis of confidence. The Spaniards under Cortés overthrew a thriving, vast, young, and vibrant civilization, though one that emphasized formal conquest and exactions substantially more than its predecessors.

4

Early Civilizations of the Andes

THE ANDEAN REGION ALSO HAS A HISTORY OF GREAT CIVILIZATIONS THAT rivals Mesoamerica, but with its own distinctive characteristics. Overall, little evidence to date indicates much contact between these two high culture zones of the Americas, and what interaction did occur seems to have been both brief and circumscribed. The Andean region is divided into two very distinct environmental zones: the coast—quite arid except for the area where it is crossed by fast-flowing small rivers (particularly in the north); and the highlands—cold, with very steep terrain, limited access to water, and few sustained fertile, level areas. Far more than in Mesoamerica, Andean cultural history is characterized by massive irrigation systems, strong states led by powerful ruling lineages, extensive warfare, and—until the Incas—only regional empires. Also, the Andean zone experienced very limited urbanization and never developed enduring marketing systems, even though it was broken into sharply dissimilar and circumscribed ecological niches, each with its own distinctive products and craft goods. The coast produced maize, fish, and woven cotton goods. The highlands relied on potatoes, llamas (and other camelids) for both meat and transport, and woven woolen items.[1]

Our knowledge of precontact Andean cultures is markedly inferior to that of Mesoamerica. Far fewer archaeological excavations have been conducted throughout the area, and for many years most of these concentrated on Incan sites to the neglect of earlier civilizations. This relative disregard of previous cultures was abetted by the Incan empire's official doctrine that it was the first major civilization in the Andes and that its empire had brought most improvements to the subject provinces. This, of course, very much contrasts with Mesoamerica, where the Aztecs were quick to acknowledge previous civilizations and even stressed that they were the heirs to the Toltecs.

Also, the Andean peoples never developed a tradition of writing, or any sort of glyphic mnemonic system, that might assist understanding of their histories and dynamics. Few Inca *quipus* (clusters of knotted cords that recorded numbers and amounts of various items) survive. In any case, these quipus, which date from the immediate precontact era, record only certain types of information (primarily harvests, herds, and community censuses).

Agriculture came early to the Andes, perhaps even earlier than in Mesoamerica. Although cultivation had already emerged in the southern highland valleys by 5500 B.C., with maize, potatoes, squash, beans, and quinoa under cultivation by 4550 B.C., the first civilizations of some scale with developed cultural styles appeared along the coast. Societies in this narrow strip of land (no more than sixty miles wide) began to produce cotton textiles around 3000 B.C. and were producing finely woven, artistically sophisticated cloth by 2500 B.C. In fact, in the Andes, cotton weaving preceded pottery, which did not appear until 1800 to 1500 B.C.

Shortly after 1000 B.C. the Chavín cult, the first culture to have widespread influence, emerged in the northern highlands. Chavín de Huantar, the largest ceremonial site, is not an elaborate complex, but its cultural style pervaded the northern highlands and coastal zone until it faded rapidly around 300 B.C. Unlike the Olmecs, its contemporary culture in Mesoamerica, the Chavín cult seems never to have had an empire of any size or to have functioned as a trading or manufacturing center. More likely, it devised a compelling religious tradition whose belief system and icons spread throughout the northern region. No evidence of destruction or invasion accompanies the fall of the Chavín culture. Rather, its disappearance was followed by a diversity of local influences, with no dominant culture appearing for about a millennium.

These nucleated cultures, however, created new styles and motifs, some of incredible achievement and beauty. Perhaps the finest example is the Mochica civilization, which occupied the north coast from A.D. 200 to 700. Its finely honed pottery depicted human activities, ceremonies, and the doings of the gods in a realistic manner. The Mochica are also the first known Andean society to organize into an identifiable state, although they never created a capital city of any size. There are some indications that they had carved out a small empire, however, and demanded periodic labor service from subject societies. The ecological niche the Mochica occupied along the north coast provided them with an abundance of foods, but so isolated them that they could not readily undertake imperial expansion. The Nazca of the southern coast (contemporaries of the Mochica) crafted lovely polychrome pottery, but they are best known for the massive complex called the Nazca lines, which are discernible only from an aerial perspective. These designs commonly extend over several hundred yards and depict animals and shapes that are also portrayed on their pottery. The purpose of these lines is still unknown.

TIAHUANACO AND HUARI:
PRECURSORS OF THE INCAN EMPIRE

About A.D. 400, two significant cities emerged in the Andean highlands: Tiahuanaco near Lake Titicaca in Bolivia and Huari near the modern city of Ayacucho in Peru's south-central highlands. The relationship of the two entities remains unclear and hotly debated, but each city ruled over empires of unprecedented size. Huari may have been some sort of dependent of Tiahuanaco, as ruler of its northern province or the like, but it also may have been quite independent. These cities do not appear to have been in prolonged conflict against each other, and Huari's empire, which emerged later (A.D. 600–800), was shorter-lived than that of Tiahuanaco and incorporated some of Tiahuanaco's primary cultural representations.

At its height around A.D. 600, Tiahuanaco's center contained only twenty thousand to forty thousand inhabitants. The people constructed raised fields surrounded by canals to increase their food production to support the large urban population. The ceremonial center was laid out in a grid pattern, and its buildings were aligned with the cardinal directions (north, south, east, and west). Great labor went into the site's construction; much of the stone, quarried on the other side of the lake, had to be transported by boat. Artistic depictions from that time indicate that the elite may have sponsored festivals that included substantial drugs and alcohol consumption to entice labor services from commoners and inhabitants of conquered provinces. (By the time of the Incas, such festival sponsorship was common throughout the Andes.)

Tiahuanaco's outlying centers were not built in heavily populated zones, but rather in sparsely inhabited areas, seemingly occupied by migrants from the region surrounding the capital. This pattern of colonization and direct exchange within the ethnic group—as opposed to markets and commercial interaction—was also characteristic of the greater Andean region during Incan times. Stuart J. Fiedel has commented on this subject: "The history of Andean highland-based empires, from Tiahuanaco to the Incas, can be interpreted as essentially an effort by mountain-dwellers to ensure a steady supply of low-altitude products, that is, to achieve *vertical control*."[2] Huari is a much less impressive ceremonial site than Tiahuanaco, and it too prospered by extensive use of agricultural engineering, in its case terracing and irrigating mountainsides, especially at lower, more temperate elevations. The Huari seem to have used quipus as recording devices and to have constructed compounds in outlying provinces rather than just to base officials in the communities of subject peoples.

Craig Morris and Adriana von Hagen have summarized the overall impact on the Incan empire of these two contemporary centers:

> Tiwanaku [sic] and Wari [sic] both collapsed as states, but the changes they made in the ways the Andean region was managed became part of a heritage of special strategies to exploit rich but widely dispersed resources. Based on moving people to directly exploit resources, these strategies almost certainly were not new, but they represented an evolution of the ways highland communities had probably exploited their world for centuries. Tiwanaku and Wari added two new elements to these old and fundamental principles. On the one hand, new or greatly expanded technologies of land reclamation allowed previously underutilized regions to become increasingly productive. On the other hand, a set of social mechanisms allowed the states to mobilize and invest ever-larger numbers of laborers in projects of reclamation and production for the states....For decades, many archaeologists have attributed the expansion of Tiwanaku, and especially Wari, to military conquest. While conflicts and military skirmishes were undertaken by both states, the fundamental factors were economic, backed by new and more sophisticated religious and political ideologies.[3]

After the near simultaneous decline of Tiahuanaco and Huari around 1000, no highland empire with influence greater than local importance arose until the emergence of the Incas in the early fifteenth century. These four centuries marked a time of actual cultural regression in the highlands, as people abandoned virtually all cities in the area and dispersed into rural hamlets.

The Kingdom of Chimor:
The Final Coastal Civilization

The coastal zone witnessed only one other culture of importance until the Incan expansion: the Chimú civilization based around the capital city of Chan Chan. The city emerged around A.D. 800 in the Moche Valley, which earlier had been the location of the Mochica culture. The Chimú did not begin to subordinate other peoples until about 1200. Ultimately, they controlled other river-valley societies stretched along 625 miles of coast, probably more through their economic preeminence—and unrivaled ability to provide sometimes scarce comestibles and craft goods—than through formal conquest. They exercised no direct control over the adjacent highlands. When taken by the Incas in 1465, Chan Chan, with a population of twenty-five thousand to fifty thousand, was divided into ten compounds, each one formed on the elevation of a new monarch and his lineage. The city was heavily dependent on a massive and complex system of surrounding irrigation canals. In fact, the Incas later conquered Chan Chan without actually invading it by threatening to cut it off from this system. Typical of cities and empires in the Andean world, Chan Chan did not serve as a commercial center; it did employ some thousands of artisans, however, whose goods were allocated and distributed by state functionaries. Craig Morris and Adriana von Hagen have stated:

> The ability to dispense valued prestige goods was a major source of the political power of leaders. At its height, Chimor [the kingdom of the Chimú] seems to have been able to command enormous quantities of high-status goods through its state-managed production. Chimú rulers probably redistributed these goods effectively to enhance their power.[4]

THE INCAN EMPIRE:
THE FIRST EXTENSIVE ANDEAN CIVILIZATION

After 1438 the Incan empire spread unexpectedly and rapidly throughout the highlands, probably abetted by the political disintegration and cultural stagnation that had plagued the region over the preceding several hundred years.[5] But it did not stop there; rather, the empire incorporated the coastal lowlands as well and became the first empire in the Andean zone to include both areas. The Incas saw both their culture and their empire as unprecedented and themselves as the fount of civilization. They belittled the contributions of earlier peoples to the Andean way of life, depicting themselves as the originators of virtually every achievement in the region. Only in recent decades have scholars been able to overcome this near-exclusive Incan focus and begin to appreciate the vibrancy of other Andean societies, both previous and contemporary to the Incan empire.

For a few hundred years before their emergence in 1438, the Incas persisted as an undistinguished culture in their capital city of Cuzco. Their rise commenced with their successful repulsion of an attack on

Cuzco by a neighboring group, the Chanca. This defense was led by the monarch's younger son, who after the victory renamed himself Pachacuti ("Earthshaker" or "World Transformer" in the Quechuan language) and repudiated both his father and elder brother, who had been chosen to succeed to the throne. The greater part of the empire was assembled over the next forty years or so, during the lifetime of Pachacuti and his favorite son and successor, Topa Inca. The subsequent two emperors enjoyed only a modicum of success in expanding the empire, and it hardly grew over the decade preceding Pizarro's capture of the emperor Atahuallpa in 1532.[6]

The empire's stagnation is reflected in the lopsidedness of the imperial boundaries when the Spanish arrived—some twenty-five hundred miles from north to south, but only a few hundred miles from the Pacific coast to the jungles of the Amazon headwaters. The Incas had subjugated virtually every sedentary society in the Andean zone, but they had experienced little success against the nonsedentary and semisedentary peoples to the east and south. The terrain in these areas was much harsher and the resources generally scanty. But most important, the local societies were culturally quite foreign to the Incas and to the greater sedentary Andean culture zone. They were hit-and-run, extremely mobile tribal peoples, who made heavy use of projectile points in combat and were next to impossible to subordinate. (The Spanish would experience similar failure in offensives against them for several centuries.) Thus the Incan empire may well have reached its attainable boundaries.

Incan culture and trade goods also did not proliferate far beyond the imperial borders. This is in sharp contrast with Mesoamerican civilizations, which for more than a millennium and a half traded with and otherwise significantly influenced societies well outside of the common culture zone itself. Of course, the peoples who interacted with these civilizations were themselves already agricultural to a considerable extent and found both the trade goods and cultural inputs to be compatible with their aspirations and ways of life. Such was not the case in South America, where sharply distinct environmental zones militated against peoples living in rather comparable styles, and where the steep and difficult highlands separated most of the interior societies from the high cultures along coastal Peru. Nor had long-term and prosperous empires in the highlands preceded that of the Incas. The peoples lying beyond the highlands had no tradition of beneficial cultural absorption from that region to draw upon when the Incan empire suddenly arose (most of the empire was assembled in forty years). And, of course, the Incas did not endure all that long—less than a century—before they were overthrown. The consequence is that few Incan-influenced sites, cultural symbols and practices, or trade goods have been found outside the imperial zone.

The Incan empire seems to have faced significantly fewer rebellions than did its counterparts in Mesoamerica, probably due to the peace that the empire successfully imposed after several centuries of fruitless warfare in the region, and particularly to the considerable material improvement it engendered through its extensive agricultural engineering projects. The Incas promoted vast expansion of terrace construction, accompanied by the excavation of elaborate irrigation systems. No evidence indicates famines or significant shortages during the Incan era, unlike in Mesoamerica, where several famines struck during the heyday of Aztec expansion. In addition, the Incas used conquered peoples as members of their imperial armies and rewarded them concomitantly.

The Incas also elaborated on the ancient Andean practice of migration and colonization by ethnic groups (colonists were known as *mitimae*) to perform some highly useful social engineering. Craig Morris and Adriana von Hagen have observed:

> ...Andean groups sometimes deployed colonies of their members to exploit resources of ecological zones at some distance from their primary living area. Expanding this custom, the Inka [sic] often moved people to faraway locations convenient for the aims of the state and its rulers. Under this policy, known as *mitmaq*, they were able to move people for strategic reasons, locating rebellious or uncooperative groups among more loyal peoples, or placing loyal groups in unstable regions. Many of the population movements had economic reasons as well. Newly claimed lands, such as those in the Urubamba Valley, were populated by experienced maize farmers, while other groups, such as herders, went to grassland regions where state herds were being developed to increase cloth production.[7]

The peoples of the Andean world had traditionally provided labor service (called *mit'a*) for their ethnic lords (*curacas*) and any imperial rulers, but, unlike in Mesoamerica, they did not complement this with delivery of tribute goods. Rulers displayed the reciprocal character of these obligations by storehousing surplus commodities and distributing them in times of shortages and by celebrating and festing the workers who came to work on their lands or on public works projects. The Incas simply expanded on these practices and the tradition of reciprocity. On this subject, Friedrich Katz has commented:

> In the same way that the village elder had maintained and provided for all the peasants who had worked for

him, the Inca state provided for and maintained all those who laboured for it. Since the assignment of labour planned for the village community was always looked upon as a joyful occasion, to be celebrated and introduced with festivities, the Inca state also instituted great celebrations at the beginning of each assignment of labour and rewarded and maintained all those who reported for work. Nevertheless, the similarity of the forms could not conceal the radical differences that existed between limited labour voluntarily undertaken for a village elder and the organised labour for a state bureaucracy based on compulsion. Above all the similarity of form could not conceal the fact that in a village the work which the members carried out was at least paid back by the chieftains in the shape of benefits that were clear for all to see. In the Inca state a part of the enormous revenues was used for purposes that also benefited the village communities: aid in emergencies, the installation of large irrigation systems, religious ceremonies, various kinds of gifts. Nevertheless, the greater part always went to the maintenance of the Inca, his court, his relatives, above all the enormous Inca bureaucracy, and for financing Inca wars.[8]

The Incas developed a road system spanning more than fourteen thousand miles, radiating in four directions from Cuzco, and extending throughout the empire. (The Incas called their empire *Tahuantinsuyu*, the land of the four quarters, with the dividing lines converging in Cuzco.) In the case of roads, the Incas once again adopted and greatly expanded on an existing Andean tradition. The system was not intended for common travel but rather for the use of imperial messengers (*chasquis*), who were based in waystations several miles from each other along the roads (*tambos*), to facilitate the movement of the imperial army throughout the region and for packtrains of llamas carrying supplies.

The ability of the Incan imperial bureaucracy to develop public-works projects and to organize people and the delivery of goods to regional administrative headquarters is perhaps epitomized in the construction of several "artificial" cities in rather unpopulated areas along the road system. The best known of these is Huánaco Pampa, in the north-central highlands nearly four hundred miles from Cuzco, inhabited by a small permanent population of administrators who supervised this district. It included nearly four thousand structures, however, for the benefit of the great many people who periodically visited the city for state ceremonies. It had about five hundred warehouses holding maize and other comestibles and also large containers of *chicha* (maize beer), which was consumed in vast amounts at celebrations. A compound of about fifty residences served as the living and working space for celibate women, who dedicated their lives to preparing food, drink, and cloth for the invited guests. All of this, of course, demonstrated the grandeur and power of the Incas, while continuing the Andean tradition of reciprocity and celebration between rulers and subordinates. The local communities near Huánaco Pampa enjoyed little connection with it or impact from it, however. An artificial construction in the region, Huánaco Pampa functioned to extol and benefit the empire, not to integrate or service the local economies. With the Spanish conquest, Huánaco Pampa was soon abandoned, while the traditional local societies remained intact and functioning as they had before the center was erected.[9]

Despite the tremendous amount of agricultural development and construction of roads and administrative centers that the Incas carried out, the Andean zone remained substantially rural in character with negligible urbanization. The capital city of Cuzco, for example, reached at most sixty thousand inhabitants, and it was not connected to a series of substantial provincial headquarters of the conquered peoples. Nigel Davies has commented about the capital: "Even the central part, though not without a somber splendor, probably lacked true monumentalism in the form of great vistas such as might enhance the grandeur of an imperial city. Notable also for their absence were the teeming markets to be found in most great capitals."[10]

The vast majority of people continued to live in widely separated communities of fewer than a thousand inhabitants. Exchange of products from one environmental zone to another was characteristically conducted within individual lineage groups, which would station branches in a diversity of settings to ensure access to otherwise scarce commodities. (This system has been termed "vertical archipelagos.") Most production of craft goods for exchange was done under the auspices of the local or imperial government, which then took control of the items and distributed them as rewards or tributes. No class of long-distance merchants existed, nor were there thriving regional market centers, as was the case throughout Mesoamerica.

From the rise of the Incan empire under Pachacuti, and probably even earlier, the empire was considered divine, a child of the sun god. Despite this, the empire proved tolerant of the local religious traditions of those it conquered. In the same way that it lacked sizable cities, the Andean region had few ceremonial sites of much scale and elaboration. Cuzco, for example, itself did not contain an extensive religious compound, and priests did not have the identity and prominence that they held in Mesoamerica. Although there were certainly large-scale religious rituals and especially important gods and locations, overall, religious belief and practice was highly localized (even within ethnic groups). Individuals and groups displayed primary devotion to *huacas,* places and natural objects that had revealed their sacredness.

The Andean zone lacked the writing systems, the heritage of successive civilizations with the same or similar gods and religious traditions, and the high-status, learned priests of Mesoamerica. Hence, even the Incas could not subordinate local beliefs and practices within a single, overarching religious framework. This is reflected in the scholarly community's weak understanding of (and relative inattention to) Andean cosmology, especially when compared with the region's labor systems, infrastructural improvements, and imperial arrangements.

The Incas made remarkable advances in medicine and surgery. They performed trepanning operations and had some rudimentary knowledge of anesthesia. The Andean peoples were also well advanced in metallurgy, making good use of copper and bronze in addition to gold and silver. They had a much simpler and less abstract knowledge of mathematics than did the Mesoamerican cultures. Their understanding of astronomy was likewise quite basic when compared with that in the other great sedentary civilization zone. They did not intertwine their ritual and annual calendar and seem not to have had a well-elaborated understanding of the solar year, at least one that has been clearly articulated in any of the early chronicles.

5

Important Attributes of Sedentary and Semisedentary Societies

THE ADVANCED CIVILIZATIONS THAT DOMINATED THE PRECONTACT HISTORIES of Mesoamerica and the Andean zone shared certain significant social, economic, and political characteristics. Although most of our information on these attributes pertains to the Aztec and Inca eras, it appears to be quite ancient in nature and to have marked earlier civilizations as much as those encountered by the Spanish.

CHARACTERISTICS OF SEDENTARY IMPERIAL CIVILIZATIONS

Fictive kinship-based communities that held land in common had arisen as the fundamental social institution as early as the first civilizations in Mesoamerica and the Andes, probably sooner. These entities—termed *calpullis* in Nahuatl (the most common language in late precontact Mesoamerica) and *ayllus* in Quechua (the most common language in the Andes)—proliferated until the coming of the Europeans, despite the immense transformations that these vast culture zones underwent, particularly dramatic increases in population and the elaboration of society with the expansion of elites and of nonagricultural occupations. In a city, practitioners of a certain craft or occupation often clustered in a single neighborhood and formed such a group. These structures did not retard the migration of peoples (and segments of societies) that was so characteristic of both culture zones. Migrants were routinely absorbed and new calpullis and ayllus were formed out of combinations of different peoples in frontier zones and periods of flux.

Though a residential community based on fictive kinship, the calpulli or ayllu was not a clan; marriage was permitted within and outside the group, with the latter apparently more common, and the infliction of injury against a member did not demand revenge from the group. The community could constitute an entire village, part of a village, or a small district in a city. Its population was substantially undifferentiated, except for the local leader, who embodied the community's ideals, distributed land among the individual households, adjudicated local disputes, and represented the community as a political unit. Each calpulli and ayllu had its local god and worship site. Each functioned as a military unit under the command of its own officers. Each delivered labor service to the local leader and through him, to the larger provincial and imperial authorities who commonly controlled the community. The role of leader was generally passed down from father to son, but competence and commitment to the larger group were required or modifications might be made to the succession. Strict primogeniture did not govern succession to the throne, even among the imperial lineages.

In the Andes the ayllu even facilitated the location of a kin group's branches in distinct ecological zones for the production and exchange of commodities. In her study of the indigenous province of Huarochirí, Karen Spalding has noted:

> That broader relationship between people defined as kin made it possible for households to throw the net of their holdings wider, cultivating land at different altitudes, in as many of the microecologies to which the larger group held access as possible. In a real sense, access to kin, defined as people who could—and would—act to protect a person's interest, could be equated with wealth....This structure of support explains how it was possible for ayllu members to lay effective claim to lands scattered over a broad area. Despite the fact that the lands claimed by ayllus were frequently widely separated—even to the point of being in different river valley systems—there is considerable evidence that ayllu members continued to claim, and cultivate, lands spread over a wide area throughout the Spanish colonial period. The remnants of that pattern can be found today.[1]

The centrality of these descent groups seems to have declined over the centuries as these sedentary societies expanded and became more complex. The ruling elites and their imperial administrators existed outside of this structure, as did priests and some other high-ranked groups in some situations. Nonetheless, the calpulli or ayllu was not an outdated vestige at the time the Americas came into contact with Europe. In fact, they remained fundamental structures in indigenous life throughout the colonial period and, in many rural areas, they still exist in present-day Latin America.

These fully sedentary peoples embraced a variety of landholding patterns at the same time. In addition to the communally held lands that characterized these kin groups, noble lineages had their own lands that were worked by dependent retainers, and periodically by members of these kin groups performing their rotary draft labor service. In fact, the nobility of an expanding imperial power benefited disproportionately from conquests, generally taking lands from subjugated provinces for their own use. Lands were also set aside for the maintenance of imperial administrators, provisioning of the military, and the upkeep of religious temples and their priests. Commoners performing their obligatory rotary labor service saw to the cultivation and harvest of crops. Finally, these peoples had the concept of privately owned land well before the arrival of Europeans. For example, individuals who had usufruct to land held by the kin group around the community center might also have had private holdings situated farther away from the village.[2]

In these sedentary societies men dominated work in the fields, although women seem to have assisted them at such particularly busy times as planting and harvesting. Women operated the households, often clustered into residential compounds, and processed foods, took care of food storage, and handled the crucial task of weaving cloth. These cultures were highly patriarchal, practicing a doctrine of masculine priority in politics and household governance. The senior man in any family lineage generally headed up the family compound in which other members of his family resided. If the compound grew overlarge, it would spin off a new one focused around another man of seniority in the descent group. A couple did not necessarily move into the husband's family compound, though it frequently did. Sometimes they moved into the wife's family compound, and more rarely, into a distant relative's. Men and women measured their descent lines through both their mother's and father's lineages.

Recent scholarship has demonstrated that royal families were crucial to the designation and maintenance of both provincial and imperial rulers. Far from being omnipotent, the ruler needed staunch support from his lineage, and flawed or ineffectual leaders seem at times to have been removed from their posts by the disgruntled descent group and replaced. Perhaps the most direct example of this practice is in the early colonial history of Fray Diego Durán, which was substantially derived from an indigenous Mexican chronicle. It addresses the ineffectual five-year reign of the Aztec emperor Tizoc in the late fifteenth century:

> During this time Tlacaelel [a revered elderly counselor within the royal family] urged Tizoc to finish the building of the Great Temple because only a small part had been constructed. But before the work could begin, members of Tizoc's court, angered by his weakness and lack of desire to enlarge and glorify the Aztec nation, hastened his death with something they gave him to eat. He died in the year 1486, still a young man.[3]

Nor was ascension to the throne generally assigned to the ruler's eldest son. Rulership more commonly passed from one brother to another until all members of a generation who were considered competent to rule by the lineage had been selected. The position then passed down a generation, more often from uncle to nephew than from father to son.[4] Because noblemen in these societies had multiple wives (primarily to establish political alliances), the royal family generally had a number of contenders — and much rivalry — for the throne. Although the dynasty maintained the public posture that the late ruler himself chose his successor before his demise, each transition seems to have been preceded by considerable rivalry and coalition-building among the major contenders and their supporting factions. Particularly among the Incas, the victor sometimes had to execute disgruntled losers or face organized revolts.[5] Nonetheless, the elements comprising the royal lineage could be expected to stand together when faced with an outside enemy or challenge that threatened their collective preeminence.

None of the imperial civilizations in either zone sought to transform the cultural practices or traditional identity of the ethnic provinces they subordinated. The local nobility retained their stature and authority so long as they accepted their imperial subordination. In fact, despite periodic visits from tax collectors and regional administrators, ethnic lords functioned as indispensable leaders and organizers under the imperial systems. They assembled their commoners for labor service and operated the delivery of tribute and the storehousing of foodstuffs for the local people and for the imperial army, if it was on campaign. Few military garrisons were erected, because they were very expensive to maintain and most of the citizen-soldiers were agriculturalists and craftsmen who had to return to work. The imperial centers even incorporated defeated peoples as part of their armies, allowing them to fight as distinct units under their own commanders.

Pedro de Cieza de León, perhaps the most astute Spanish commentator in Peru in the decades following the conquest of the Incas, described the Incan mode of invasion as follows:

> They always arranged matters, in the commencement of their negotiations, so that things should be pleasantly

and not harshly ordered. Afterwards, some Incas inflicted severe punishments in many parts; but formerly, it is asserted on all sides, that they induced people to submit by great benevolence and friendliness. They marched from Cuzco with their army and warlike materials, until they were near the region they intended to conquer. Then they collected very complete information touching the power of the enemy and whence help was likely to reach them, and by what road. This being known, the most effective steps were taken to prevent the succour from arriving, either by large bribes given to the allies, or by forcible resistance. At the same time, forts were ordered to be constructed on heights or ridges, consisting of circles with high walls, one inside the other and each with a door. Thus if the outer one was lost, the defenders could retire into the next, and the next, until refuge was taken in the highest. They sent chosen men to examine the land, to see the roads, and learn by what means they were defended, as well as the places whence the enemy received supplies. When the road that should be taken and the necessary measures were decided upon, the Inca sent special messengers to the enemy to say that he desired to have them as allies and relations, so that, with joyful hearts and willing minds they ought to come forth to receive him in their province, and give him obedience as in the other provinces; and that they might do this of their own accord, he sent presents to the native chiefs. By this wise policy he entered into the possession of many lands without war. In that case, he gave orders to his soldiers that they should do no harm or injury, nor commit any robbery or act of violence; and if there were not sufficient provisions in the province, he ordered that it should be sent from other parts.[6]

Nor were the conquered peoples required to abandon their gods, distinctive cultural practices and styles, or language. They were expected to accept the victors' supreme god into their pantheon, however, something seemingly accepted without rancor, as that god had demonstrated his efficacy through the success of the conquest. The language of the conquering power spread widely throughout the empire, at least among the provincial authorities and commercial interests. Likewise, the craft goods and cultural styles of the imperial centers tended to be diffused more broadly, though their acceptance seems not to have been directly imposed.

From the earliest days, warfare among the sedentary societies was characterized by close combat between massed armies using shock weapons (clubs, swords, and spears) rather than prolonged long-distance exchanges of projectiles. The armies were under the strict control of their leaders and moved in close, disciplined formations. The death or capture of a commander put his unit out of action. Warriors stressed the capture of their individual opponents on the battlefield instead of slaying them. Certainly in Mesoamerica, this was the primary way that military glory was attained.

Warfare had a strong protocol, with declarations of war preceding actual invasions. The opposing sides commonly engaged in combat in open areas far away from cities and other settlements. They neither slew noncombatants nor, in general, devastated crops or settlements. Few walled cities existed in the early Americas, although in the Andes larger cities sometimes did have adjacent fortresses. As noted earlier, the systematic sacrifice of war captives was restricted to the Aztecs of Mesoamerica.

In his thorough study of warfare in ancient Mesoamerica, Ross Hassig has noted the following general patterns:

> Four major expansions—Olmec, Teotihuanaco, Toltec, and Aztec, the last three imperial—were crucial in creating the Mesoamerican culture area. Although they varied in their initial rise, each society enjoyed a military advantage in their expansions. First, each was numerically superior. Second, they enjoyed superior weaponry. Third, they enjoyed an organizational advantage, combining their superiority in numbers with both old and new weapons to create larger and better trained, armored, and integrated armies. Fourth, they enjoyed a logistical advantage based first on better foodstuffs—retoasted tortillas—and later on, a superior organization that permitted resupply en route. Behind each lay an economy dependent on the export of manufactured goods and the import of exotic goods and raw materials. Conquests were easiest and most numerous when they were asymmetrical, pitting opponents with major differences in power, military equipment, tactics, and organization. When and where conflicts were relatively symmetrical, little political expansion occurred.[7]

Intact imperial armies were impregnable against attacks by hunting-and-gathering people—except for looting raids along the periphery—and these nomadic peoples were only able to overthrow sedentary societies when those societies were already in disarray. But in similar fashion, the great imperial armies enjoyed little luck when they invaded the mountainous, desert, or tropical terrains of tribal peoples. The natives would simply withdraw before them, while harassing the attackers with ambushes and arrow fire, and select new leaders to replace any captured or slain.

THE GREAT NUMBER AND VARIETY OF SEMISEDENTARY PEOPLES

Although the sedentary imperial peoples of the Americas attained the highest civilizations, semisedentary peoples (who practiced a less intensive form of agriculture because of environmental limitations) inhabited a far greater part of the territory on the two continents. Although these hundreds of ethnic and language groups depended heavily on agriculture for sustenance, because of harsher terrain, less fertile land, and technology restrictions, they had to move their settlements periodically to nearby fresh land and to supplement cultivation with hunting, fishing, trapping, and the like to round out their dietary needs. A major consequence of this lesser agricultural output and the need to move periodically was a substantially decreased population density as compared with fully sedentary peoples.

In North America virtually the entire region south of the Great Lakes and the St. Lawrence River and east of the Mississippi River consisted of semisedentary peoples. In fact, given the general expanse of forests throughout this region before the coming of Europeans (with the significant exception of the floodplains of the Mississippi and Ohio Rivers), the peoples living in this region shared a broadly comparable material culture and way of life and are thus commonly referred to as Eastern Woodlands Indians, although they retained a diversity of ethnicities and languages. West of the Mississippi, the land was much less forested and of much lower quality, given the technology that the inhabitants could then apply and the dearth of draft animals. Therefore, most of the peoples in its vastness were hunters and gatherers (with the important exception of some societies along the Pacific coast that thrived from fishing and some limited agriculture). Nomadic bands also inhabited the plains and arid country of central and southern South America.

From the Yucatán Peninsula southward, Central America was inhabited by such semisedentary societies (the Mayan civilization of the Yucatán lowlands had fragmented into semisedentary existence around A.D. 900), as was roughly the northern half of South America east of the Andes, encompassing great parts of the modern countries of Bolivia, Brazil, Colombia, and Venezuela.[8] The vast Amazon River basin contained many such peoples (it was much more densely populated than today), with its numerous communities eating well from a diet based on manioc and fish.⁹ Even Chile and Paraguay included substantial numbers of semisedentary peoples, though they were surrounded by marauding hunting-and-gathering tribes.

The Tainos, the primary ethnic group of the larger Caribbean islands, lived under chiefdoms (themselves ranked) and in towns that could number several thousand inhabitants. Clearly influenced by Mesoamerica, their communities were organized around plazas and included ball courts similar to those on the mainland. Like the peoples of the Amazon and coastal Brazil, they thrived on a manioc- and fish-based diet, with maize constituting only a secondary foodstuff.¹⁰

Although all semisedentary peoples practiced some form of agriculture, the actual level of dependence varied from one society to another, according to the local environment's characteristics. Furthermore, those semisedentary societies living close to sedentary imperial cultures were often affected by these more advanced civilizations. Those groups farther away from such zones and closer to nomadic bands lived a much more rudimentary existence. The natural environments of several zones were particularly favorable for producing bountiful agriculture, especially when coordinated with effective human intervention. These zones yielded societies with substantial populations, some level of urbanism, and significant ceremonial sites. This was the case in two distinct regions in North America over the span of several centuries roughly seven hundred to eleven hundred years ago — the American Southwest and the floodplain of the Mississippi and Ohio Rivers.

The American Southwest

Maize has been successfully cultivated in the American Southwest since at least some three thousand years before modern times and possibly some centuries earlier. The peoples in this arid zone made use of the occasional river beds and erratically sufficient rainfall to establish sedentary agricultural villages, some of which persisted for hundreds of years. Agriculture thrived in this vast region only through massive human intercession in the construction of terraces, check dams, reservoirs, and irrigation complexes. Its inhabitants were too dispersed to be organized into long-enduring political hierarchies, but they did compose several enduring culture zones with considerable manufacture of basketry and pottery of notable artistic achievement as well as rare minerals (particularly turquoise). By about A.D. 700 the Hohokam, Mogollon, and especially the Anasazi cultures had developed to some scale. (It is difficult to date their phases and the emergence of their periods of florescence, for the process was very gradual and not marked by abrupt shifts in either the types of goods produced or the methods of manufacture.)

The Anasazi's achievements were the most notable. Between 900 and 1250 their population was at its greatest, and the people were clustered in and around several sites, the most developed of which were Chaco Canyon and Mesa Verde. Chaco Canyon contained eight pueblos, with four others located along its rim. The largest, Pueblo Bonito, contained 650–800 rooms housing several thousand people, and the residences rose four to five storeys around a central plaza. Some 200–350 small villages ran along the canyon's southern side. People may have spent much of their time in these small settlements and moved to the central pueblos for important rituals. The Chaco Canyon pueblos maintained colonies as far as one hundred miles away and constructed wide roads that ran in a straight line for more than fifty miles. At its height, the population of the entire Anasazi zone approached one hundred thousand.

The Anasazi routinely conducted trade with central Mexico, their turquoise items being especially prized. Craft goods from Mexico have been found in numerous Anasazi pueblos. Certain Mexican beliefs and icons were widely adopted by the Anasazi as well. Around 1200, however, the focus of trade with central Mexico seems to have shifted southward, well out of the Anasazi zone.

Starting about the same time, the Anasazi seem to have begun to suffer from decreased agricultural production, probably from a combination of lower rainfall and erosion. Warfare increased, probably between pueblos rather than against invaders. People began to migrate away from the great sites, and by 1300 a number had settled in the Rio Grande valley far to the east, where they mixed with groups coming into the area from other directions. This mixture produced the Pueblo peoples. By 1400 the Anasazi culture had collapsed.

The Pueblo peoples numbered at least one hundred thousand by 1600 and were dispersed among roughly 135 communities, none of which had a population of more than three thousand. This rather small number of people was further divided into four distinct language groups. Stuart J. Fiedel has offered the following description of larger Pueblo culture:

> Pueblo societies were basically egalitarian, without major differences in wealth or status of individuals. The population was usually divided into exogamous clans, each named for a totemic animal or plant, and each possessing its own fetishes and secret rituals....Most Pueblo societies were matrilineal and matrilocal; that is, women owned the houses, fields, and stored crops, and clan membership was passed on in the female line of descent. A married man left his own family to live with his wife

and her mother and sisters. However, men dominated the political and religious spheres. The governing body in secular matters was a council of elders; a council of priests tended to religious matters.[11]

THE FLOODPLAIN OF THE MISSISSIPPI AND OHIO RIVERS

In the eastern part of the continent the floodplain of the Mississippi and Ohio Rivers supported a number of mound-building cultures starting as early as twenty-five hundred years ago. These sites are classified as the Adena (500 B.C.–A.D. 100), Hopewell (100–400), and Mississippian cultures (700–1500). The Eastern Woodlands Indians apparently adopted maize cultivation under Mississippian influence around 900 to 1000, although they had been cultivating less nutritious seeds for hundreds of years. The primary Mississippian site, Cahokia, probably achieved the status of a state at its peak between 1050 and 1250, when it supported a population of around thirty thousand in the city proper and as many in its hinterland. It fully commanded forty additional settlements, established some colonies of its own, and traded widely throughout the vast center of North America. Mississippian culture, although not its predecessors, seems to have been affected by Mesoamerica. On this subject, Stuart J. Fiedel has remarked:

> The standard plan of Mississippian communities—platform mounds capped by temples and élite residences, arranged around an open plaza, and often surrounded by numerous dwellings—is one of the features that have given rise to theories of a strong diffusionary influence, perhaps even migration, from Mesoamerica. Additional traits that hint at a Mexican connection are maize cultivation and certain religious symbols and artistic motifs....[12]

This culture had disintegrated by the time Europeans arrived, but it influenced the cultures throughout a substantial region in the American Southeast, yielding what is called the "Southern Cult." The Natchez and Creek are prominent among the peoples so affected.

AGRICULTURAL PRACTICES

Aside from such major but exceptional cases, semisedentary societies did not generally carry out permanent improvements to increase agricultural productivity, such as terraces and raised fields. Rather, they depended almost exclusively on swidden (or "slash and burn," as it is often called) agriculture. This involved community members cutting down and then burning the brush and small trees in a certain area. The area was then suitable for cultivation, with the ash providing fertilizer. Generally, such a field provided three to five years of good harvests before output drastically declined. The community then moved to another promising site a short distance away and carried out the same procedure. The process continued time after time within a circumscribed zone until the earliest cultivated area had become once again fully overgrown and hence suitable for cultivation. This "circuit" usually consumed no more than twenty-five years. Thus the community's mobility took place within a well-delimited region and within boundaries that the community, and its neighboring communities, recognized (which is not to say that a neighboring society might not encroach upon it or raid it). These periodic village migrations, then, took on a predictable character, following a certain route that would take the inhabitants to fields that they or their parents had worked a generation before.

Social, Cultural, and Political Practices

A great variety of social and cultural practices developed among the many semisedentary societies scattered across such vast and distinctive territories. Among the Eastern Woodlands peoples of North America, only women actually cultivated the crops, generally working in gangs in the fields and assisting each other with child care, while men worked to clear and burn down fields. Perhaps as a consequence of their central role in producing the bulk of nutrition for their societies, women enjoyed considerable political power. For example, women had to approve policies and diplomatic arrangements worked out by chiefs before they could be implemented. Lineage was measured through the female line, and residence in longhouses and family compounds was organized around one's affiliation to the senior female who headed the residential complex. This central figure also dictated men's work and participation in blood feuds on behalf of her clan. Elder women could demand warfare and likewise refuse to sanction it. When daughters married, their husbands moved into their mother's longhouse with them. In some societies divorces were common and easily arranged. Unmarried sons remained in their mother's abode. Men spent much time away from their villages and families, as they devoted themselves to hunting, trapping, diplomacy, and warfare—all of which took them into the uninhabited countryside.[13] Incidentally, such arrangements were known in South America as well, particularly among the Guaraní of Paraguay, where women dominated agriculture, headed lineages, organized work and warfare, and had considerable voice in political deliberations.

The decreased nutrition provided by this way of life, together with the required periodic movement of the community, dictated that semisedentary peoples had a significantly lower population density than the fully sedentary peoples. Furthermore, they had somewhat less occupational and social elaboration. Few if any full-time craftsmen or other specialists could achieve economic self-sufficiency; most of the time virtually everyone was an agriculturalist (or spouse of an agriculturalist). Lacking many craft items or local commodities, trade among communities was rudimentary and regular markets as they existed in Mesoamerica were hardly known.

Few political structures and loyalties existed above the village level. In fact, the community often endured a certain instability, as lineages within it might spin off to found their own hamlets. With the exception of several debatable cases that benefited from enhanced agricultural productivity, many semisedentary societies in the Americas never organized themselves into states with true political structures and institutions. When the Europeans arrived, the most complex alliance among semisedentary peoples was the Iroquois Confederation of Five Tribes, who saw themselves as sharing a common ethnicity with their neighbors. But this confederation, at the time less than two hundred years old, functioned primarily as a nonaggression pact among the participants. It provided neither for coordinated military operations in the event of warfare against other peoples nor for a council of representatives from the five tribes to set policy.[14]

Communities among semisedentary peoples tended to be led by chiefs, who spoke for their people and led rituals and war parties but who lacked political authority. Instead, these villages—striving to maintain internal cohesion—practiced consensus politics, in which virtually every family had to agree to any important decision if it was to be effective. These chiefs, therefore, could not demand tribute payments or labor service from their people. No permanent nobility existed. Rather, chiefs were selected for specific diplomatic or military campaigns, and their authority did not persist after the campaign's conclusion. Nor could the offspring of chiefs anticipate succeeding their fathers.

Although warfare against other lineages, communities, and sometimes entire tribes was common (perhaps endemic) among semisedentary peoples, conquest, long-term subordination, and the exaction of tribute or labor service was unknown. The conditions necessary for long-lasting empires were totally lacking among these societies. Groups initiated warfare to right a perceived wrong or injury inflicted on them by outsiders. (Because all the inhabitants in a given region produced essentially the same basic goods and few if any specialized or luxury items, the possibility of plunder did not incite attacks.) Similar to sedentary imperial cultures, warfare among semisedentary peoples typically involved few casualties and did not emphasize the destruction of the opponent's community or the slaughter of noncombatants. Combat usually involved small bands of men fighting at a distance from settled areas. The rugged countryside lent itself to ambushes and quick retreats. War parties suffering even a few casualties commonly withdrew from the field. Greater prestige was accorded to capturing an opponent rather than killing him, even though the commonality of bow-and-arrow warfare made combat inherently lethal.[15]

Captives brought back to the village were usually ritually tortured to death (in the process, supposedly righting the wrong inflicted) or were—somewhat less often, it seems—adopted into the lineage to replace the person whose death engendered the warfare in the first place. Many societies in both North and South America assimilated outsiders—and sometimes entire remnant communities or tribes—into their midst, a practice often witnessed (and probably more necessary) when the coming of Europeans brought more deadly warfare and disease, resulting in the decimation of entire villages and tribes.

The Population of the Americas on the Eve of European Contact

It is best to consider the size of the native population of the Americas before the arrival of Europeans in light of the impact that agriculture has on population densities. In this view, it is obvious that sedentary peoples enjoyed much greater populations than did semisedentary ones; in turn, semisedentary societies greatly surpassed nonsedentary ones. Likewise, the substantial urbanization that characterized at least Mesoamerica reflects high population densities.

The population of both continents probably totaled between sixty-five million and seventy-five million in the late fifteenth century, comparable to (if not slightly larger than) the population of Europe west of Russia at the same time. The area with the largest population was central Mexico, with up to twenty-five million, the Aztec empire containing the majority of them. The Andean region, with more rugged country breaking up its agricultural expanses, contained twelve million to fifteen million, with a high percentage part of the Incan empire. The Caribbean and Central America (including the Yucatán) were inhabited primarily by semisedentary societies, each yielding populations of six million to seven million. South America outside of the Andes contained mostly semisedentary peoples in its northern and central parts and nonsedentary cultures more in the south, totaling about nine million to ten million. North America contained perhaps seven million inhabitants, five million of those in what became the United States and an additional two million or so in what became Canada. Of these, perhaps two-thirds lived as semisedentary peoples east of the Mississippi River—the Eastern Woodlands Indians—and in the agricultural communities of the

American Southwest. The peoples of the western plains were, of course, largely dependent on hunting for their subsistence.[16]

Two notable factors help to explain the significant population density achieved by the native peoples of the Americas. First, maize was the primary grain cultivated heavily in parts of both continents. It routinely yielded more calories per acre than did any of the grains in the Old World at that time. Its nutritional value was further enhanced by the manner in which it was prepared and by its common combination with beans and squash. Second, after being cut off from the Old World more than ten thousand years earlier, the Americas had avoided exposure to some of the worst epidemic diseases that regularly ravaged other parts of the world.[17]

6

Conclusion

By the fifteenth century the native peoples of the Americas were divided into dozens of language groups and hundreds of ethnicities. This was not a new development. Humans have been in the Americas for at least twelve thousand years and perhaps more than twenty thousand years. And the earliest civilizations—each having a distinctive cultural style, significant ceremonial sites, and complex social and political arrangements—emerged at least three thousand years ago. Despite this great variety, the Native Americans shared certain broad characteristics, depending on whether they were sedentary, semisedentary, or nonsedentary societies. These were neither immutable nor hard-and-fast classifications, for certain cultures fell into interstitial categories—such as the Tainos, who were organized into permanent communities governed by chiefdoms, although they were far from achieving the governmental structures and cultural sophistication of the peoples of central Mexico. And groups in such areas as the Yucatán Peninsula and the American Southwest changed their mode of production over the centuries as they responded to ecological changes and political disruptions.

Mesoamerica and the Andean region, the areas of highest cultural achievement, witnessed a succession of civilizations before producing those of the Aztecs and the Incas—the best known civilizations, as they were encountered by Europeans in the early sixteenth century. Despite their accomplishments, however, they were short-lived by the standards of their culture zones. In most fundamental ways, the Aztec empire did not represent a signal advance over the preceding civilizations. The Incas, though, had integrated the greater Andean region like no earlier empire had done. Nonetheless, they used many longstanding, widespread practices as they expanded their authority.

Cultural styles and societies themselves—intact or remnants thereof—moved widely throughout the Americas. Mesoamerican influence reached far into North America at different times, and peoples from northern Mexico migrated almost continuously into the area of high culture represented by central Mexico. Tremendous, and often carefully planned, migration took place in the Andes as well. Cultural exchange likewise occurred between the highland and the tropical Amazon societies, although far less is known about its dimensions. Widespread trade and movement also characterized the semisedentary and nonsedentary peoples of North America. Many had changed their primary area of residence or made major cultural adaptations in the last several centuries before contact with the Old World. Although ancient in many ways, the various Native American cultures were not ossified but rather dynamic and vital, with their own distinctive perspectives and concerns, when Europeans reached the two continents.

Notes

2. CLASSIC CIVILIZATIONS OF MESOAMERICA

1. Charles C. Di Peso, "Prehistory: Southern Periphery," in *Southwest*, ed. Alfonso Ortiz, Vol. 9 of *Handbook of North American Indians*, ed. William C. Sturtevant (Washington, D.C.: Smithsonian Institution Press, 1979), 160.

2. Fray Bernardino de Sahagún, *Florentine Codex – General History of the Things of New Spain, Book X*, quoted in Nigel Davies, *The Ancient Kingdoms of Mexico* (Harmondsworth, England: Penguin Books, 1983), 112.

3. Stuart J. Fiedel, *Prehistory of the Americas* (Cambridge: Cambridge University Press, 1987), 287.

4. Michael D. Coe, Dean Snow, and Elizabeth Benson, *Atlas of Ancient America* (New York: Facts on File Inc., 1986), 118.

5. Based substantially on Mayan language documentation, a major advance in our understanding of colonial Mayan society is Matthew B. Restall, *The Maya World: Yucatec Culture and Society, 1550–1850* (Stanford, Calif.: Stanford University Press, 1997).

3. THE END OF THE CLASSIC PERIOD

1. Di Peso, "Prehistory: Southern Periphery," 159.

2. Di Peso, "Prehistory: Southern Periphery," 159.

3. Nigel Davies, *The Toltecs: Until the Fall of Tula* (Norman: University of Oklahoma Press, 1977); *The Toltec Heritage: From the Fall of Tula to the Rise of*

Tenochtitlán (Norman: University of Oklahoma Press, 1980); and *The Aztec Empire: The Toltec Resurgence* (Norman: University of Oklahoma Press, 1987).

4. Joyce Marcus, *Mesoamerican Writing Systems: Propaganda, Myth, and History in Four Ancient Civilizations* (Princeton. N.J.: Princeton University Press, 1992), 42.

5. Michael D. Coe, *Mexico,* 3d ed. (New York: Thames and Hudson Inc., 1984), 145.

6. Nigel Davies, *The Ancient Kingdoms of Mexico* (Harmondsworth, England: Penguin Books, 1983), 195.

4. Early Civilizations of the Andes

1. An excellent brief comparison of the cultural histories of Mesoamerica and the Andes remains Friedrich Katz, *The Ancient American Civilizations* (New York: Praeger Publishers, 1974), 94–95.

2. Fiedel, *Prehistory of the Americas*, 331.

3. Craig Morris and Adriana von Hagen, *The Inka Empire and Its Andean Origins* (New York: Abbeville Press Inc., 1993), 122–23.

4. Morris and von Hagen, *The Inka Empire*, 138.

5. "Inca" initially signified only the title of the emperor but later came to refer to the entire ethnic group.

6. Katz, *The Ancient American Civilizations*, 295–96.

7. Morris and von Hagen, *The Inka Empire*, 159.

8. Katz, *The Ancient American Civilizations*, 291–92.

9. Morris and von Hagen, *The Inka Empire*, 166–69.

10. Nigel Davies, *The Incas* (Niwot: University Press of Colorado, 1995), 106.

5. Important Attributes of Sedentary and Semisedentary Societies

1. Karen Spalding, *Huarochirí: An Andean Society under Inca and Spanish Rule* (Stanford, Calif.: Stanford University Press, 1984), 30.

2. This was first demonstrated in compelling fashion in S. L. Cline, *Colonial Culhuacan, 1580–1600: A Social History of an Aztec Town* (Albuquerque: University of New Mexico Press, 1986), chap. 8.

3. Fray Diego Durán, *The History of the Indies of New Spain*, trans. Doris Heyden (Norman: University of Oklahoma Press, 1994), 307.

4. The most precise and detailed description of this process is provided in Durán, *The History of the Indies*, 309–10.

5. Discussion of some of these revolts by dissident Incan factions is in Thomas C. Patterson, *The Inca Empire: The Formation and Disintegration of a Pre-Capitalist State* (Providence, R.I.: Berg Publishers Ltd., 1991), 113, 119–23. See also Father Bernabe Cobo, *History of the Inca Empire*, trans. and ed. Roland Hamilton (Austin: University of Texas Press, 1979), 118–19, 121, 137, 152–53, 163–66.

6. Pedro de Cieza de León, *The Second Part of the Chronicle of Peru*, trans. and

ed. Clements R. Markham, The Hakluyt Society, First Series, no. 68 (New York: Burt Franklin, n.d.), 47-48.

7. Ross Hassig, *War and Society in Ancient Mesoamerica* (Berkeley: University of California Press, 1992), 178.

8. Two excellent books depict the structures and culture of the Yucatec Maya on the arrival of the Spanish: Inga Clendinnen, *Ambivalent Conquests: Maya and Spaniard in Yucatan, 1517-1570* (Cambridge: Cambridge University Press, 1987); and Nancy M. Farriss, *Maya Society under Colonial Rule: The Collective Enterprise of Survival* (Princeton, N.J.: Princeton University Press, 1984).

9. Fiedel, *Prehistory of the Americas*, 192-200, offers a cogent consideration of the early emerging agricultural and ceramic traditions of the Amazon and Orinoco basins.

10. Irving Rouse, *The Tainos: Rise and Decline of the People Who Greeted Columbus* (New Haven, Conn.: Yale University Press, 1992), 9-17.

11. Fiedel, *Prehistory of the Americas*, 216.

12. Fiedel, *Prehistory of the Americas*, 245.

13. These practices have been best documented and described within the Iroquois Confederation. See Anthony F. C. Wallace, *The Death and Rebirth of the Seneca* (New York: Vintage Books, 1972), chap. 2; and Daniel K. Richter, *The Ordeal of the Longhouse: The Peoples of the Iroquois League in the Era of European Colonization* (Chapel Hill: University of North Carolina Press, 1992), chap. 1 and 2. They can be compared with the other cultures depicted in Helen C. Rountree, *The Powhatan Indians of Virginia: Their Traditional Culture* (Norman: University of Oklahoma Press, 1989); and J. Leitch Wright Jr., *Creeks and Seminoles: The Destruction and Regeneration of the Muscogulge People* (Lincoln: University of Nebraska Press, 1986).

14. Matthew Dennis, *Cultivating a Landscape of Peace: Iroquois-European Encounters in Seventeenth-Century America* (Ithaca, N.Y.: Cornell University Press, 1993), chap. 2.

15. Patrick M. Malone, *The Skulking Way of War: Technology and Tactics among the New England Indians* (Baltimore, Md.: Johns Hopkins University Press, 1993), chap. 1.

16. The literature on the precontact population of the Americas and on subsequent rates of depopulation and recovery is voluminous and of high quality. Despite strong arguments on the subject, the trend over the past thirty years or so is for a substantial increase in the accepted minimum population that existed. A recent, particularly compelling argument for a large population in Mexico is Robert McCaa, "Spanish and Nahuatl Views on Smallpox and Demographic Catastrophe in Mexico," *Journal of Interdisciplinary History*, 25, no. 3 (winter 1995), 397-431. Two broadly conceived works on the topic are William M. Denevan, ed., *The Native Population of the Americas in 1492* (Madison: University of Wisconsin Press, 1976); and Russell Thornton, *American Indian Holocaust and Survival: A Population History since 1492* (Norman: University of Oklahoma Press, 1987).

17. A superior collection of writings on disease among the precontact native peoples (who suffered from a number of serious ailments but not from epidemics) and on depopulation is John W. Verano and Douglas H. Ubelaker, eds., *Disease and Demography in the Americas* (Washington, D.C.: Smithsonian Institution Press, 1992).

Bibliography

Berdan, Frances F. *The Aztecs of Central Mexico: An Imperial Society.* New York: Holt, Rinehart & Winston, 1982.

Brody, Jerry J. *The Anasazi: Ancient Indian People of the American Southwest.* New York: Rizzoli International Publications Inc., 1990.

Bruhns, Karen Olsen. *Ancient South America.* Cambridge: Cambridge University Press, 1994.

Calloway, Colin G. *The Western Abenakis of Vermont, 1600–1800: War, Migration, and the Survival of an Indian People.* Norman: University of Oklahoma Press, 1990.

Clendinnen, Inga. *Ambivalent Conquests: Maya and Spaniard in Yucatán, 1517–1570.* Cambridge: Cambridge University Press, 1987.

———. *Aztecs: An Interpretation.* Cambridge: Cambridge University Press, 1991.

Cline, S. L. *Colonial Culhuacan, 1580–1600: A Social History of an Aztec Town.* Albuquerque: University of New Mexico Press, 1986.

Coe, Michael D. *Mexico.* 3d ed. New York: Thames and Hudson Inc., 1984.

———. *The Maya.* 4th ed. New York: Thames and Hudson Inc., 1987.

Coe, Michael D., Dean Snow, and Elizabeth Benson. *Atlas of Ancient America.* New York: Facts on File Inc., 1986.

Davies, Nigel. *The Ancient Kingdoms of Mexico.* Harmondsworth, England: Penguin Books, 1983.

———. *The Incas.* Niwot: University Press of Colorado, 1995.

Dennis, Matthew. *Cultivating a Landscape of Peace: Iroquois-European*

Encounters in Seventeenth-Century America. Ithaca, N.Y.: Cornell University Press, 1993.

Di Peso, Charles C. "Prehistory: Southern Periphery." In *Southwest*, ed. Alfonso Ortiz. Vol. 9 of *Handbook of North American Indians*, ed. William C. Sturtevant. Washington, D.C.: Smithsonian Institution Press, 1979.

Farriss, Nancy M. *Maya Society under Colonial Rule: The Collective Enterprise of Survival*. Princeton, N.J.: Princeton University Press, 1984.

Fiedel, Stuart J. *Prehistory of the Americas*. Cambridge: Cambridge University Press, 1987.

Hassig, Ross. *Aztec Warfare: Imperial Expansion and Political Control*. Norman: University of Oklahoma Press, 1988.

———. *War and Society in Ancient Mesoamerica*. Berkeley: University of California Press, 1992.

Hyslop, John. *The Inka Road System*. New York: Academic Press, 1985.

———. *Inka Settlement Planning*. Austin: University of Texas Press, 1990.

Jennings, Francis. *The Founders of America*. New York: W. W. Norton & Company, 1993.

Josephy Jr., Alvin M., ed. *America in 1492: The World of the Indian Peoples before the Arrival of Columbus*. New York: Alfred A. Knopf Inc., 1992.

Katz, Friedrich. *The Ancient American Civilizations*. New York: Praeger Publishers, 1972.

Keatinge, Richard W., ed. *Peruvian Prehistory*. Cambridge: Cambridge University Press, 1988.

Lockhart, James. *The Nahuas after the Conquest: A Social and Cultural History of the Indians of Central Mexico, Sixteenth-Eighteenth Centuries*. Stanford, Calif.: Stanford University Press, 1992.

Lucena Salmoral, Manuel. *America 1492: Portrait of a Continent 500 Years Ago*. New York: Facts on File Inc., 1990.

Malone, Patrick M. *The Skulking Way of War: Technology and Tactics among the New England Indians*. Baltimore, Md.: Johns Hopkins University Press, 1993.

Marcus, Joyce. *Mesoamerican Writing Systems: Propaganda, Myth, and History in Four Ancient Civilizations*. Princeton, N.J.: Princeton University Press, 1992.

McCaa, Robert. "Spanish and Nahuatl Views on Smallpox and Demographic Catastrophe in Mexico." *Journal of Interdisciplinary History* 25, no. 3 (winter 1995): 397-431.

Merchant, Alexander. *From Barter to Slavery: The Economic Relations of Portuguese and Indians in the Settlement of Brazil, 1500-1580*. Baltimore, Md.: Johns Hopkins University Press, 1942.

Milanich, Jerald T. *Florida Indians and the Invasion from Europe*. Gainesville: University Press of Florida, 1995.

Morris, Craig, and Donald E. Thompson. *Huánuco Pampa: An Inca City and Its Hinterland*. London: Thames and Hudson Inc., 1985.

Morris, Craig, and Adriana von Hagen. *The Inka Empire and Its Andean Origins*. New York: Abbeville Press Inc., 1993.

Murra, John. *The Economic Organization of the Inka State*. Research in Economic Anthropology, Supplement 1. Greenwich, Conn.: JAI Press Inc., 1980.

Pollard, Helen Perlstein. *Taríacuri's Legacy: The Prehispanic Tarascan State*. Norman: University of Oklahoma Press, 1993.

Restall, Matthew B. *The Maya World: Yucatec Culture and Society, 1550–1850*. Stanford, Calif.: Stanford University Press, 1997.

Richter, Daniel K. *The Ordeal of the Longhouse: The Peoples of the Iroquois League in the Era of European Colonization*. Chapel Hill: University of North Carolina Press, 1992.

Rountree, Helen C. *The Powhatan Indians of Virginia: Their Traditional Culture*. Norman: University of Oklahoma Press, 1989.

Rouse, Irving. *The Tainos: Rise and Decline of the People Who Greeted Columbus*. New Haven, Conn.: Yale University Press, 1992.

Salisbury, Neal. *Manitou and Providence: Indians, Europeans, and the Making of New England, 1500–1643*. New York: Oxford University Press, 1982.

Schroeder, Susan. *Chimalpahin and the Kingdoms of Chalco*. Tucson: University of Arizona Press, 1991.

Service, Elman R. *Spanish-Guaraní Relations in Early Colonial Paraguay*. Ann Arbor: University of Michigan Press, 1954.

Sharer, Robert J. *The Ancient Maya*. 5th ed. Stanford, Calif.: Stanford University Press, 1994.

Spalding, Karen. *Huarochirí: An Andean Society under Inca and Spanish Rule*. Stanford, Calif.: Stanford University Press, 1984.

Stern, Steve J. *Peru's Indian Peoples and the Challenge of Spanish Conquest: Huamanga to 1640*. Madison: University of Wisconsin Press, 1982.

Verano, John W., and Douglas H. Ubelaker, eds. *Disease and Demography in the Americas*. Washington, D.C.: Smithsonian Institution Press, 1992.

Wallace, Anthony F. C. *The Death and Rebirth of the Seneca*. New York: Vintage Books, 1972.

Wright Jr., J. Leitch. *Creeks and Seminoles: The Destruction and Regeneration of the Muscogulge People*. Lincoln: University of Nebraska Press, 1986.

Zuidema, R. Tom. *Inca Civilization in Cuzco*. Austin: University of Texas Press, 1990.